STRINGER'S
LAST STAND

A Play

by

STAN BARSTOW
&
ALFRED BRADLEY

SAMUEL   FRENCH

LONDON
NEW YORK TORONTO SYDNEY HOLLYWOOD

FOR AMATEUR PRODUCTION ENQUIRIES

UNITED KINGDOM AND WORLD
EXCLUDING NORTH AMERICA
plays@samuelfrench.co.uk
020 7255 4302/01

Each title is subject to availability from Samuel French,
depending upon country of performance.

CHARACTERS

Bessie Stringer
Gladys Stringer
Luther Stringer
Bob Carter
Jack Harper
Marjorie Mather (*née* Stringer)
Carol Stringer
Ann Fairchild

The action of the play passes in the working-class living-room of the Stringers' house in a small Yorkshire industrial town

Time - the present

ACT 1

SCENE 1

The Stringers' living-room. Early evening

The room is comfortable and there is no squalor or clutter. Everything is clean and neat, but well used

Bessie Stringer, a woman in her late twenties, is finishing laying the table for the evening meal. Gladys, Bessie's mother, a woman in her middle fifties, is in the kitchen, cooking. She appears in the doorway

Gladys Have you got the table laid, Bessie?

Bessie I'm on with it now.

Gladys Well, don't take all day. Your father'll be here any minute.

Bessie And he doesn't like to be kept waiting. I know. (*She moves a vase of plastic daffodils from the table to the sideboard*) Mam, do we have to have these?

Gladys Have what?

Bessie These flowers. They look awful. They don't convince anybody.

Gladys They look real to me.

Bessie You can get fresh daffs at Marstons for two bob a bunch.

Gladys Aye. And I can get two pounds of onions for two bob an' all.

Bessie It's not as if you ever change them. It's spring all the time in this house from April through to Christmas.

Gladys I don't know what you're going on about. There's your father now. Look sharp, I'll get the stew out.

Gladys goes back into the kitchen as Luther comes into the house by the back door

Luther (*off*) Get out from under me feet.

Gladys (*off*) Now what's the dog done to you?

Luther (*off*) He wor in me way. When I come home from a hard day's work I don't want to have to stride over that fat useless lump. Is it ready?

Gladys enters with the stewpot which she sets in the middle of the table

Bessie What's up with him, then?

Gladys You might well ask. For goodness' sake don't get his back up tonight, Bessie. I've had a splitting head all day. (*Calls*) It's ready when you are.

Luther enters. He is not a big man but as he adjusts his shirtsleeves he

*makes it seem a characteristically aggressive gesture. He looks as though
he's about to square up to the world*

Luther Stew, is it?

Gladys And dumplings.

Luther Aye, all right.

Gladys Don't say you don't fancy it. You were asking only the other day
when we were going to have it again.

Luther I said "all right", didn't I? What do you want, a song and dance?

Gladys and Bessie exchange looks as Gladys serves on to Luther's plate

He'll have to go y'know.

Gladys Who'll have to go?

Luther That dog.

Gladys You'll have to take him, then, 'cos I shan't.

Luther It's no kindness to him, letting him linger on like that.

Bessie Poor old Spot.

Gladys I don't know 'at he's in any pain.

They all settle down to eat

Luther He's half blind and his coat's coming out.

Gladys As long as he's warm and comfortable.

Bessie Our Marjorie's little 'uns think the world of him.

Luther Don't be so soft, Bessie. There's not one of 'em taken a blind bit
o' notice of him in ages. All he does nowadays is lie on that mat all day.
An' he's beginning to smell.

Gladys He never is!

Luther You don't notice because you're in the house all day.

Gladys Have you noticed it, Bessie?

Bessie Well, sometimes I've wondered if he doesn't, just a bit.

Luther It's tragic to see him, when you think back to how he used to be.
At one time he'd be off after every bitch on heat inside three or four
mile.

Gladys Stopping out in all weathers and coming back soaked to the skin.

Luther Bleedin', many a time, when he'd had to scrap for it.

Gladys Aye.

Luther Take owt on, he would. Any size, any breed. Now t'poor old
bugger's got all on to drag himself out into t'yard.

Gladys He's warm and comfortable and he gets fed regular. Just hope
you're as well looked after when you're in his condition.

Luther I hope I don't hang on long enough to get in his condition. I wish
I thought somebody'd have t'kindness to put me quietly to sleep.

Gladys You can talk like that now. But life's sweet.

Luther More than you can say for these dumplings.

Gladys I don't know why. I've made 'em like I always do.

Luther Then you must have been heavy-handed. Dumplings need a light
hand.

Gladys Is there owt else you can find fault with while you're at it?

Luther I'm telling you 'at dumpling's is sad so's you'll know for next time.

Gladys If they'd been perfect you'd never have said a word, I suppose.

Luther If I expect me grub to be perfect you've nobbut yerself to blame.

Bessie I think that's a compliment, Mother.

Gladys Or t'nearest he'll ever get to one.

Luther It seems I'm in t'wrong whatever I say.

They all eat through a longish pause

Bessie Did our Marjorie take Neville to the hospital?

Gladys Yes. The specialist said there was nowt much wrong. He gave her some drops for his ear and told her to take him back in a fortnight.

Luther If you ask me t'strain's runnin' out there.

Gladys She's your daughter, Luther.

Luther I don't mean on her side. Our Marjorie's as strong as an ox. She has bairns like a chicken lays eggs. I'm talkin' about Jim. He's nobbut size o' sixpennorth o' copper. I wonder sometimes where he gets the strength. No wonder he looks pasty.

Gladys Luther!

Luther And it's not as if they've been wed all that long. There's time for another dozen the way he's shapin' up. I don't know why they can't lie fallow for a bit. You'd think he'd ha' found out what causes it be now.

Gladys Luther, I wish you wouldn't talk like that in front of our Bessie.

Luther She's a grown woman, isn't she? If you'd talked a bit more to our Marjorie she might not be where she is now. Five bairns in as many years is too much of a good thing.

Gladys Well, the youngest is nearly three now.

Luther Aye, it's about time she were stubbing her toe again.

Gladys If it comes to that, what about our Carol? There's eight years between our Bessie and her, so you weren't so clever.

Luther Our Carol was a bit of a surprise, but she's a grand healthy lass. And clever with it. I reckon she could tell us all a thing or two.

Gladys It's to be hoped she's got common sense an' all. I can't rest with her away at university and television showing nothing but drugs and student riots, and demonstrations about everything under the sun.

Luther That's protest, lass. They're trying to change the world. If we'd changed it long since they wouldn't have to bother. Bloody good luck to 'em, I say. Except it'd do a few of 'em good to get a haircut an' do a hard day's work. Anyway, I sometimes think our Bessie's got most o't' common sense 'at war handed out to this family. She's biding her time. Though I do think she might be leaving it a touch late if she's got any real intention.

Gladys Our Bessie 'ull get married when she's ready.

Luther Aye.

Bessie Don't mind me, just go on talking about me as if I'm not here.

Luther You're not getting any younger, Bessie.

Bessie I'd be a freak if I did, wouldn't I? Nobody gets younger.

Luther Aye, but it's not the same with men. Age doesn't matter so much. With a lass it's different. By the time you reach thirty your chances are getting slim. If a chap gets to thirty without gettin' wed they say he's lucky.

Bessie They say he's not natural.

Luther Aye, they say that as well. But a feller can allus get a wife. Look at these old chaps who marry lasses of twenty. It doesn't often happen t'other road round.

Gladys You've got some big ideas about yerselves, you men.

Luther That's where you're wrong. I feel sorry for women, sometimes. Give 'em a good education and all the opportunities in the world and they still feel they've lost out if they don't get a husband.

Bessie Well, like me mam says, I shall get married when I'm ready, and not before.

Luther As long as you're not ready on your own.

Bessie I'm not short o' choice.

Luther You'll get shorter as folk get fed up o' waitin' for thee.

Gladys She *is* engaged, Luther.

Luther Aye.

Bessie Did Bob say anything about coming round tonight, Dad?

Luther No, he didn't.

Bessie Didn't he mention it at all?

Luther I haven't spoken to him all day.

Bessie Well, that's funny, an' him workin' right next to you. Is there something up, or what?

Luther You might say that. They've sent him to Coventry.

Gladys But that's miles away. Will he get home week-ends?

Bessie What d'you mean, they've sent him to Coventry?

Luther Just what I say.

Bessie But whatever for?

Luther I didn't work yesterday, did I?

Bessie No, you didn't, but . . .

Luther I didn't work because we had a one-day token strike in support o't'wage claim. I didn't work an' none o' t'other union members worked —bar Bob. He went in as usual.

Bessie And you mean none of you's talking to him just because of that?

Luther (*sarcastically*) Aye, just because of that.

Bessie Well, it's downright childish, that's what it is. Nobody talking to him because he worked yesterday.

Luther Look here, Bessie: what do you do wi' a lass when you've no time for her?

Bessie Well, I . . .

Luther Come on, be honest about it.

Bessie Well, I suppose I don't have anything to do with her. But . . .

Luther That's right. An' when a lot o' men feel that way about a chap it's called sending him to Coventry.

Gladys You don't mean to say *you've* fallen in with it, Luther?

Luther I have that. I'm wi' t'men.

Bessie But Bob's my fiancy.

Luther Aye, an' my future son-in-law, I'm sorry to say.

Gladys I must say it does seem a shame 'at you should treat your own daughter's fiancy like that, Luther.

Luther Now look. Bob's a member o' t' union. When t'union negotiates a rise in wages, Bob gets it. When it gets us an improvement in conditions, Bob gets that an' all. But when t'union calls for strike action what does Bob do? He goes to work as usual. Now I don't like a chap what does a thing like that. An' when I don't like a chap I have no truck with him.

Bessie I'll bet nobody gave him a chance to put his side of it.

Luther He's got no side. There's only one side to this for a union member. He should ha' struck wi' t'rest on us.

Bessie (*muttering*) Well, that's a proper mess. An' now I don't know whether I've to go an' meet him or he's coming here, or what . . .

Luther I shouldn't think he'll have the cheek to show his face in here tonight.

There is a knock on the back door. It opens and Bob's voice is heard

Bob (*off*) Hello! Anybody in?

Bessie It looks like you can think again!

As Bessie goes through into the kitchen Luther takes the evening paper and opens it, lifting it so that he is hidden behind it. Bob enters with Bessie. He is a man in his middle twenties, a year or two younger than Bessie

Bob 'Evening, Mrs Stringer.

Gladys Hello, Bob. Our Bessie was just wondering whether you'd be coming or not.

Bob Oh? (*To Bessie*) Your dad's told you about it, then.

Bessie Aye, he has. And I told him how childish I think it is. Like a pack o' schoolkids, they all are.

Bob (*muttering*) A flock o' sheep, more like. All fallin' in together.

Luther (*lowering the newspaper*) Aye, all together. How else do you think a union can work?

Bessie Oh, you'll talk to him now, then?

Luther I'm askin' him a question. How else does he think a union can work?

Bob I don't know an' I don't care. I'm fed up wi' t'union an' everybody in it.

Luther That's a lot o' men. An' there's a fair number of 'em fed up wi' thee, lad. Anyway, happen tha'll not be bothered wi' it for much longer.

Bob How d'ye mean?

Luther I mean they'll likely call for thi card afore long.

Bob Well, good riddance. I never wanted to join in the first place.

Luther Why did you, then?

Bob Because I couldn't have the job unless I did. I was forced into it.

Luther Aye, an' for why? Because we don't want a lot o' scroungers an' wasters gettin' t'benefits while we pay t'subscriptions.

Bob Who's callin' me a scrounger? Don't I do as good a day's work as the next man? An' better, if it comes to that.

Luther Aye, tha can work, I'll give thee that. But tha hasn't t'common sense tha war born wi'.

Bob Sense! I've enough sense to think for meself an' make up me own mind, when there isn't an independent man among t'rest of you.

Luther That's what I mean. All this talk about independence an' making up your own mind. They like it, y'know. It's playin' right into their hands.

Bob Whose hands?

Luther The bosses' hands. They like chaps 'at's independent: fellers 'at don't agree with anybody. They can get 'em on their own an' they haven't as much bargaining power as a rabbit wi' a ferret on its tail.

Bob Ah, you're fifty year out o' date. Look, here we are with the cost of living up an' up. We've got to stop somewhere. It's up to somebody to call a halt. But what does the union do but put in for another wage increase. Haven't they heard of restraint?

Luther You mean like there is on profits an' dividends, I suppose?

Bob What do you know about profits an' dividends?

Luther That's it! What *do* I know? What do you know? Nowt. We don't see any of it where we are. We have to be guided by somebody 'at knows. Somebody 'at's paid to study these things. The union leaders, lad. The union leaders. An' when they say: "Look here, lads, these fellers are coalin' in their profits an' dividends an' the cost o' livin's going up an' up and it's time we had a rise," then we listen to 'em. And when they say: "Strike, lads," we strike. At least, some of us does.

Bob Look, I believe in a fair day's work for a fair day's pay.

Luther No more na me.

Bob An' if the boss is satisfied with me work he gives me fair pay.

Luther He does if t'union's made him.

Bob He does without that, if he's a fair man. Look at Mr Crosland.

Luther Aye, let's look. I've worked for Croslands now for thirty year. I know Andrew Crosland and I knew his father afore him. Neither of 'em's ever had cause to grumble about my work and by an' large I've had no cause to grumble about them. When t'union's put in a claim they've chuntered a bit an' usually paid up. But they wouldn't if we hadn't been in force—all thinkin' an' actin' together. There's fair bosses an' there's t'other sort—that I'll grant you. But then again, there's bosses an' there's men. Men think about their wages an' the bosses think about their profits. It's business, lad. It's the system. You've got to face it they're on one side and we're on the other. An' when we want summat we've got to show 'em 'at we're all together an' we mean to have it. That's what's made us all so mad at thee. We listened to t'union and tha listened to t'bosses callin' for wage restraint.

Bob I don't listen to t' bosses. I watch the telly an' read the papers an' make up me own mind.

Luther Well tha reads t'wrong papers, then. Tha'll be tellin' me next tha votes Conservative.

Bob I don't. I vote Liberal.

Luther (*aghast*) Liberal! Good sainted aunts protect us! An' is this t'chap you're goin' to wed, Bessie?

Bessie (*chin up*) As far as I know. He's me fiancy.

Luther He'll be a fiancy wi'out a job afore long.

Bessie Why? He worked, didn't he? It's you lot they ought to sack, not Bob.

Luther (*with heavily simulated patience*) But you see, they can't sack us because there's too many of us. We've a hundred per cent shop up at Croslands an' t'men 'ull not work wi' a feller what isn't in t'union. An' your Bob won't be in t'union for much longer, or I'm a Dutchman.

Bessie Well, if that isn't the limit!

Gladys I do think it's a crying shame that a young chap should be victimized because of his principles.

Luther You keep your nose out, Gladys. This has got nowt to do wi' women.

Gladys It's summat to do wi' our Bessie. Your own daughter's young man, an' you're doin' this to him.

Luther Nay, don't blame me. There's nowt I can do about it if I wanted to.

Bessie An' you don't.

Luther I've said all I have to say.

Bessie Well, I've summat to say now. It doesn't matter what your flamin' union does to Bob. He's headin' for better things than t'shop-floor an' bein' bossed about by a pack of tuppence-ha'penny workmen.

Bob (*muttering*) Shurrup, Bessie. There's no need to go into all that now.

Bessie I think there is. I think it's time me father wa' told a thing or two. Who does he think he is, anyway? I don't suppose you know 'at Bob's been takin' a correspondence course in accountancy. An' I don't suppose you know 'at Mr Crosland himself has heard about it an' that he's as good as promised Bob a job upstairs in the Costin' Department if he does well in his exam. What do you think about that, eh?

Luther (*his voice at first quiet with menace, but rising as his feelings get the better of him*) I'll tell you what I think about it. I think you'd better take that young feller out o' my house an' never bring him back again. So he works because he doesn't agree wi' t'union policy, does he? He thinks we ought to have wage restraint, does he? He stuffs me up wi' that tale an' now you tell me 'at he's anglin' for a job on t'staff. It wasn't his principles 'at made him go in yesterday, it wa' because he wanted to keep on t'right side o' t'management.

Gladys Calm yourself, Luther. You'll have a stroke if you get so worked up.

Luther (*shouting*) I'll have a stroke if ever I see that—that scabby blackleg in my house again.

Bessie Well, you might as well know. I shall marry him whether you like it or not.

Luther Not at my expense, you won't.

Bob Come on, Bessie. Let's be off.

Bessie Aye, we'll go. You'd better see if you can control him, Mother. He's yours. This one's mine.

Bessie and Bob go out through the hall

Gladys You know, you'll do yourself no good, getting worked up like that. (*She clears the table*)

Luther Wages restraint. Think for herself. Don't be led off like a flock o' sheep. Oh, he knows how to think for hisself does that one. Y'know, I half admired him for sticking to his principles, even if I did think he was a bit daft in the head. But that one's not daft. Not him. He's crafty. He's not bothering hisself about wage restraint an' principles. He's wonderin' what Andrew might ha' thought if he'd struck wi' t'rest of us. He's wonderin' if Andrew might not have got his own back by forgettin' about that job he offered him. That's what he calls a fair boss. He knows bosses as well as t'rest of us. An' as for principle—he's got no more principle than a rattlesnake.

Gladys exits to the kitchen with the dishes to wash up

When I think of all t'football matches we've been to together . . . Well, our Bessie can wed him if she likes. She'll go her own road in the end and she's too old to be said by me. But she's no need to think he's welcome here in future. An' what's more, I won't stand for you havin' 'em in the house together when my back's turned. You hear what I'm sayin', Gladys? You're to have no more to do wi' that young man.

Gladys (*off*) Oooh! For heaven's sake, will you shut up!

The sound of a plate being violently smashed takes Luther to the kitchen doorway

Luther Have you gone daft?

Gladys enters

Gladys (*brushing past him*) I shall go daft if I listen to you much longer.

Luther That's one o' t'dinner service plates you've just chucked on t'floor.

Gladys I know it is, an' I don't care. You can pay for it out o' that rise your union's getting you. (*She picks up another plate from a pile on the dresser*) And you can pay for that one as well. (*She smashes it*)

Luther Hey, hang on! (*He scoops up the rest of the pile before she can do more damage*)

Gladys As for me, I'm going round to our Marjorie's. I shan't be making any supper, nor any breakfast tomorrow. No, nor any dinner and tea neither. I'm startin' my one-day strike now. You can look after yerself, aye, an' talk to yerself, for all I care.

Luther You're not feeling badly, are you? What's come over you?

Gladys Principle. Thirty-two year of it, saved up.

Gladys goes out through the hall

Luther Well, by bloody hell! (*He walks distractedly for a while and is irritated to find he's still clutching the pile of plates. He dumps them on the sideboard*) Well, I might as well go where I can find somebody 'at knows what I'm talkin' about.

Luther takes his jacket off the back of his chair and goes out through the kitchen, switching out the light behind him

There is a pause to denote a passage of time

The back door opens. Bessie and Bob come in. Bessie comes into the living-room and switches on the light

Bessie Come on, Bob!

Bob (*peering in*) Is it all right?

Bessie 'Course it is. There's nobody in. Me mam's probably round at our Marjorie's.

Bob It's not her I'm worried about.

Bessie Oh, we shan't see me dad for a bit. He'll have gone down to *The Greyhound*. They'll all be talking about what big men they are an' how they can make the bosses sit up. Hey, that's funny!

Bob What?

Bessie Somebody's broken one of me mam's best dinner plates. (*She begins to pick up the pieces*)

Bob I don't like the look of it. You don't think your dad's gone berserk, do you?

Bessie Not him. It's all words with him.

Bob All the same, it's a bit funny nobody's picked up the pieces. We should've gone to the pictures like I said, I don't like coming in here behind his back.

Bessie I live here, don't I? I've invited you. I can take care of me dad, don't worry. An' I'm too much on edge to enjoy the pictures tonight. I wanted a nice quiet drink and a chat.

Bob I did warn you.

Bessie But I mean—all them fellers turning their backs on you like that.

Bob It's nowt, Bessie.

Bessie It's mean and stupid and spiteful.

Bob Nay, Bessie, they're me mates.

Bessie You could have fooled me.

Bob I mean they were, like, before.

Bessie If we hadn't come out when we did I'd have given 'em a piece o' my mind. I couldn't have held back much longer, I can tell you. Grown men acting like kids. It makes your blood boil.

Bob You'd only ha' made it worse. No good getting their backs up any more. Leave 'em alone an' they'll come round in time.

Bessie Aye, in time! You read in t'papers about some chaps being in Coventry for years on end.

Bob Well then, I'll either stick it out or look for another job.

Bessie The trouble is, they'll very likely take your union card off you, then you might not find another job in a hurry. An' here's us saving up to get married. Oh, silly daft men! They cause all the trouble in the world. There wouldn't be half the bother there is if they let women run things.

Bob What makes you think that?

Bessie Because we've got more common sense, that's what.

Bob You'll have to put up for t'council, if you think that way.

Bessie I'd have to join some damn' silly political party before they'd entertain me.

Bob Anyway, let's forget it for a while.

Bessie In't it a mess, though?

Bob It'll all come out in t'wash. (*Sitting on the sofa*) Come on, sit down here.

Bessie Oh, it's all right you talking like that. What are we gunna do if you lose your job?

Bob I dunno. P'raps Mr Crosland'll give me that staff job if there's any trouble.

Bessie Aye, an' p'raps he'll let you go to save trouble.

Bob Oh, I think he's a decent sort. An' I don't think he'll let a crowd o' workmen intimidate him.

Bessie I can see *me* letting 'em if I were boss.

Bob You'd better not let your dad hear you talking like that. He'll go off the deep end. Say you're a traitor to your class, or summat like that.

Bessie Oh, I know how to stand up for me rights, don't worry. But there's a difference between that and this sort o' silly carry-on.

Bob Well, let's not let it spoil our evening, eh? (*He pats the place beside him on the sofa*)

Bessie I wonder what's on telly. (*She switches on the set and lets it warm up*) So long as it's not a play. I can't make head or tail of half of 'em. They leave you all up in the air, like that one last Wednesday, when that girl went to a funeral and that feller wanted her to be in some play but she didn't want to. Did you understand it?

Bob No, I didn't see it.

The television set warms up

Bessie Oh, look who it is. I like him. He's great. He's ageing a lot, though, lately. You'd think they'd hide it with the make-up.

Bob Nobody gets any younger, Bessie.

Bessie That's what me dad said earlier.

Bob Nobody gets any younger, and we've both aged about five minutes since I asked you to come and sit down.

Bessie puts on the standard lamp behind the TV and goes and switches off the overhead light before sitting down beside Bob. He puts his arm round her and she wriggles about a bit till she gets comfortable. They watch the TV screen

Bessie Just look at that neckline. They'll be coming on stripped to the waist before long.

Bob Roll on!

Bessie Oh, aye, I suppose you'll be all for it. It's practically every play you put on nowadays, there's some couple in bed together. I saw one the other night and this lass rolled over and showed everything she'd got. Just for a split second. If you'd been looking away you'd have missed it. But there she was, showing it all. Me mam and me were glad me dad wasn't in.

Bob They tell me there's lasses wearing see-through blouses on the streets in London.

Bessie Oh, they'll do owt down there. Our Carol's got one, though. She had it in her case last time she was home. I asked her if she'd ever worn it with nothing underneath and she said just once at a party. She didn't like it because she was cold. I told her she'd better not let me mam hear about it, nor me dad either.

Bob Is he old-fashioned about things like that?

Bessie Who, me dad? Oh, yes. He might be a bit rough in his talk now and then, but he won't have any hanky-panky. Why, what makes you ask? You've been about to places with him, haven't you?

Bob Oh, yes.

Bessie Well, you should know, then.

Bob says nothing. They watch the screen in silence for a time until Bob turns to Bessie and kisses her. She lets him, with every appearance of enjoyment, but the moment they break her eyes go back to the screen. Bob tries again and this time he moves to the edge of the sofa, letting Bessie down until she is half-lying there. He bends over close and kisses her again. It's when his hands start to roam that she breaks free and sits up

Here, just a minute! (*She goes and switches on the overhead light and smooths down her clothes*)

Bob What's up, Bessie?

Bessie A cuddle's a cuddle, but we'll have a bit less o' that.

Bob Nay, Bessie; we are engaged, aren't we?

Bessie Happen so. But I'm not one of your permissive society women. I want a wedding ring on my finger before I let a feller take liberties with me.

Bob I wasn't thinking of it as taking a liberty. I thought you were enjoying it as well.

Bessie You know what thought did.

Bob Nay, be reasonable, Bessie. You're an attractive lass and I love you. I don't know how long we'll have to wait till we can get married. Don't you ever feel . . . ?

Bessie No, I don't!

Bob I mean, don't you ever feel you'd like to?

Bessie That's for marriage. In the meantime, you'll just have to control yourself. They don't call me Alice Green.

Bob Eh? What's Alice Green got to do with it?

Bessie You used to knock about with her, didn't you? And she was always free and easy enough.

Bob How do you know she's free and easy?

Bessie I'm only telling you what's common knowledge. What about her going off on holiday with Walter Stephens?

Bob What about it?

Bessie They went to Paris. It's lucky she didn't get into trouble.

Bob What's Paris got to do with it? If you want to get into trouble you don't need to go all that way. There's plenty of people get put up the stick in—in flipping Wakefield.

Bessie You'd best not let me mam hear you saying things like that, or *she* won't want you in the house either.

Bob All I'm saying is that I always found Alice a nice enough lass. I don't know why you want to start calling her names.

Bessie I'm not calling her anything she hasn't been called before. And why did you pack up with her if you thought all that much about her?

Bob I'm not saying I think owt about her. All I'm saying is you're calling her names and I've allus found her to be a nice enough lass.

Bessie But you did finish with her, didn't you?

Bob (*hesitating*) Well, no. She finished with me, if you must know. She threw me over for a chap she met at a dance in Bradford.

Bessie So I've got to be content with Alice Green's leavings, have I?

Bob Oh, Lord! You know very well it's not like that, Bessie. I think a lot more about you than I ever did of Alice.

Bessie But all the same, she gave you more fun than you get with me, eh?

Bob I didn't bring her into this, you did. What the heck's come over you, Bessie? You're in a right mood tonight.

Bessie Aye, I am. I'm sick to death o' men, if you want to know. I'd like to bundle you all in a big cart an' tip you into the sea an' be rid of the lot of you. What with men acting like bairns and men what can't keep their hands off you, it's a wonder women have any patience left. There's our Marjorie's husband, at her till she's going to have more kids than the old woman what lived in a shoe. And me mother, putting up with me dad's domineering ways for thirty-two years. Well, I shan't have it. It'll be fifty-fifty, give an' take, when I get wed. And I shan't get wed till that's understood.

Bob It's as well we're getting to know all this. Now we can see who wants to wear the trousers.

Bessie It's not a question o' wearing trousers. But I intend to know where I stand. It's a woman's right to know what she's letting herself in for.

Bob (*meaningfully*) And a man's!

Bessie What d'you mean by that?

Bob I mean it looks as though we'd better set it all out on paper. Draw up a marriage charter, like, with all the rules an' stipulations an' agreements.

Bessie It wouldn't be a bad idea.

Bob Aye, an' what kind o' marriage would that be, with one or other of us claiming breach o' contract every other day?

Bessie It'd be a fair arrangement.

Bob Aye, I can just see it. I must be taken out twice a week, and I can claim time and a half for washing up after half-past six. And you can't come into the bedroom without clocking in. You want to get your dad to help you draw it up. It's just his cup o' tea.

Bessie You've no need to be sarcastic. It's watchin' me dad carry on 'at's made me think like this.

Bob Oh, no, it isn't. It's being his daughter, that's what it is. You think you're like your mother, but you're not. You're the spittin' image of your dad. You've no sense of humour, for a start, an' he's famous for it. You know what the lads call him at the Works, don't you? "Smiley

Stringer" they call him, because he's never been known to see a joke. You talk about him an' his pigheadedness an' domineering ways; well you want to have a good look at yourself.

Bessie If that's what you think I'm sure I don't want to hold you to anything.

Bob An' I'm sure I don't want to wed a female Luther Stringer.

Bessie Well, that settles it, then. You can go an' see if Alice Green'll have you back. I don't care. And don't think I shall have any bother finding somebody else. You're not the only pebble on my beach.

Bob I never thought I was. I mean there's—(*he pretends to think*)—and then there's . . .

Bessie (*infuriated*) Oh! Here, you can have your ring back now. I won't wear it another minute.

Bessie gets the ring off her finger, but is interrupted by a knock at the back door

An' who the heck's that?

Bessie goes through into the kitchen

Jack (*off*) Hello, Bessie.

Bessie Oh, it's you, Jack. This is a surprise. Won't you come in?

Jack (*off*) I was wondering if I could have a word with your dad?

Bessie (*off*) Well, come in, come in.

Bessie comes into the living-room with Jack Harper, a man of about thirty, following

Me dad's out just now. He'll be down at *The Greyhound*. Have you tried there?

Jack No, I thought I'd call here first seeing as how it's on me way. (*He sees Bob*) I, er—I didn't know you'd be in on your own, like.

Bessie (*staggered*) On me own? Oh, that nonsense! Well, you men! What do you think that is sitting over there? A waxwork? I suppose if Bob got up and punched you on the nose you'd reckon it hadn't happened.

Jack There's nowt personal about this, Bessie.

Bessie You can't kid me wi' that nowt personal business. O' course it's personal. An' you're all enjoying it at bottom of you. Taking your spite out on somebody you know.

Bob I don't need you to stand up for me.

Bessie I see.

Jack Nah, look here, Bessie, it's got nowt to do wi' you an' I don't want to discuss it if you don't mind. If your dad's down at t'Greyhound I'll have a walk down there an' see him.

Bessie Well, seeing as I'm on me own, I'll come with you.

Jack (*somewhat foxed*) I'll take you down an' buy you a drink with pleasure, Bessie. But I shan't be able to stop with you. I've some business to discuss with your dad, y'see.

Bessie Oh, never bother about me. I'll find somebody to talk to. An' you an' me can have a little chat on the way down. It'll be rather like old times, won't it?

Bob I hope you know what you're doing, Bessie.

Bessie Did you say something, Jack?

Jack No, I said nowt.

Bessie Funny, I thought you said something. It's stopping in on your own that does it. You start hearing things after a bit.

Bob (*to himself*) Oh, my flippin' maiden aunt! Women!

Bessie (*getting her coat*) Right, I'm ready when you are, Jack.

Jack (*putting a fag in his mouth*) Have you got a light?

Bessie I'm sorry, I don't smoke any more.

Bob takes a match from his pocket and strikes it. Jack goes towards him to take it without thinking, but before he can take advantage of the light, Bob blows it out and pockets the box

Jack Why—you!

Bob Are you talking to me?

Jack (*exasperated*) Oh, come on, Bessie.

Bessie All right. I'll leave the light on and the door open for me mother. She'll be round at our Marjorie's.

Jack and Bessie go out through the kitchen, leaving Bob alone

Bob Well, that's a right how d'ye do! What am I supposed to do now? (*He stands gazing gloomily at the television screen for a moment, then addresses it*) It's all right for you, mate, standing there singin' an' everybody lappin' it up. Have you ever had the feeling you weren't wanted? (*He switches off the set and looks round for his coat, sees it where he left it, over a chair, and puts it on. He goes to the light switch beside the kitchen door, looking through and speaking to the dog*) What do you think I should do, Spot? Should I switch the light off and slip the latch, or what? It'd be a laugh if they all found they were locked out, wouldn't it? All right, don't say owt if you don't want to. You might as well ignore me an' all. That makes just about everybody.

He turns back indecisively into the room. Just then the back door opens and women's voices are heard

Marjorie (*off*) Stop arguin', Bessie, will you, and come in.

Bob, startled, looks wildly round, then jumps behind the kitchen door

Immediately Marjorie, Bessie and Gladys come in. Marjorie carries Luther's best suit, fresh from the cleaners, on a hanger. Bessie is rather surprised to see the room empty and Bob gone so quickly, since he has not passed her outside

Gladys Where were you off to with Jack Harper?

Bessie He called to see me dad, I told him he'd be down at the pub, and then I said I'd have a walk down with him.

Gladys You set off out once with Bob. Where's he got to?

Bessie Oh, he had to go early—to do his studyin', y'know.

Gladys I see. All the same, I don't see why you have to . . .

Marjorie (*impatiently*) Look, are we going to spend t'next half hour drivellin' on about our Bessie or are we going to get down to brass tacks?

Gladys Why couldn't you have let her go about her business? I don't see 'at there's any need to bring everybody into it, Marjorie.

Marjorie Our Bessie isn't "everybody", Mam. We can't talk round at our house wi' Jim flappin' his big ears an' the kids crawling all over everything. Besides, our Bessie 'ull have summat to say about it.

Gladys I don't know what our Bessie's supposed to know about such things.

Marjorie Our Bessie's a grown woman, Mam.

Bessie That's the second time I've heard that tonight. Will somebody please tell me what I've been dragged into the house for?

Gladys (*impulsively*) I don't think . . .

Marjorie What?

Gladys Oh—nothing.

Marjorie Look, Mother, I know you must be upset but we shan't get anywhere be sweepin' it under t'carpet. We've got to talk about it an' decide what to do.

Bessie Marjorie, if you aren't the most maddening woman I know.

Marjorie Well, I can't get a word in edgeways, can I?

Bessie Do about what?

Marjorie About me dad.

Bessie What about me dad?

Marjorie pauses for full effect, glancing first at Gladys, who is looking at neither of them, then speaking in mixed tones of outrage and satisfaction at imparting a really juicy item of scandal

Marjorie He's got a woman.

Bessie (*incredulous*) You what?

Marjorie I'm telling you; he's got a woman. Or happen more than one.

Gladys Marjorie, there's no call to let your imagination run away with you. You'll have him running a harem next.

Marjorie How do we know there isn't more than one?

Gladys (*with an exasperated sigh*) Ey, Marjorie, I wish to God I'd never given you the damn suit. You're rushin' on like a bull at a gate and not givin' anybody a second to think.

Marjorie I know what I think already.

Gladys Aye, I expect you do.

Bessie What's me dad's suit got to do with—with what you just said?

Marjorie That's how I found out. Me mam asked me this morning if I'd pop me dad's suit in at that express cleaners in town while I was taking our Neville up to the hospital. She knew I'd have a while to wait so I could call for it on my way back. You know how much messing about there is. You make an appointment with a specialist for a certain time but unless you're going private there's any number of folk waitin' an' all. Then there's the tests they have to do, and then you've to take your turn in t'line again . . .

Bessie Will you get to the point.

Marjorie I'm coming to it. Well, I thought when I was in the shop 'at I'd just feel an' make sure there was nowt left in the pockets. You know how you do. I mean, me mam can't have done it, or . . .

Gladys I thought I had.

Marjorie Aye, well, you couldn't have. Anyway, I did. And it's a good job I had me back turned. If that lass behind t'counter had seen I'd not ha' known where to put me face.

Bessie But what on earth did you find?

Marjorie looks at Gladys

Gladys Nay, you wanted her in on it, you may as well tell her now.

Marjorie This. (*She takes a packet of contraceptives out of her pocket*)

The three of them stare at it

Bessie (*taking it*) "Electronically tested". What is it?

Marjorie Come on, Bessie, you can't be so green.

Gladys I don't see why not.

Bessie turns the packet over

Bessie Oh! Oh, I say! They're . . .

Marjorie Aye.

Gladys No wonder you had a funny look on your face when you called in with our Neville. I remember thinking so at the time.

Marjorie Well, I mean to say, I had to have a chance to think. Like I told you, it did cross me mind that you an' me dad might . . .

Gladys Nay, Marjorie, I'm past age where I need owt like that. An' in any case, me an' your father . . . Well, he's always been considerate since our Carol wa' born. We've managed very well without the upstairs work.

Marjorie *You* might have.

Bessie (*looking in the packet*) They do 'em up neat, don't they?

Marjorie Ugh! Mucky things. I wouldn't have one in my house.

Bessie Ey, there's only two here and there should be three.

Marjorie (*nodding*) That's right.

Bessie The old devil!

Gladys Steady on, Bessie. I'd like a bit more proof before you start calling him names.

Marjorie I don't know what more proof you want. (*She takes the packet from Bessie and waves it at Gladys*)

Gladys Well, we don't actually know, do we? Perhaps there's a simple explanation.

Marjorie Such as?

Gladys Maybe he was looking after them for a friend.

Marjorie Mother, I know it can't be a pleasant fact to face but face it you must.

Bessie What I can't understand is who'd—I mean, at his age.

Marjorie There's many a good tune played on an old fiddle.

Bessie An' when does he . . . ? It must be on t'nights he goes to t'dogs.

Marjorie Happen he doesn't go to t'dogs at all, but sees her.

Gladys Happen he takes her to t'dogs.

Bessie The old devil!

Marjorie The thing is—what are we going to do?

Bessie He wants facing with it, that's what I think.

Gladys I'd just like to know a bit more about it, that's all.

Marjorie If I didn't have Jim and t'bairns to see to I'd follow him and
see just where he does go and who he goes with.

Bessie *I'll* follow him. I'll get to the bottom of it. Me own father. My God!
When I think of all the years he's laid the law down an' browbeaten all
of us!

Marjorie The best years of me mam's life, them were.

Bessie Aye, an' now they're all thrown back in her face.

Marjorie I think it's disgustin'.

Bessie I think men are disgustin'.

Gladys Nay, Bessie.

Marjorie No, Bessie, you can't lump 'em all together.

Bessie I can if I want to.

Gladys Nay, Bessie, your dad's allus brought his money home an' seen
'at everything wa' right here.

Marjorie An' you'd never find Jim doing a thing like this.

Bessie Your Jim's got enough on his plate at home, if you ask me.

Marjorie What d'you mean be that?

Bessie I mean if anybody thinks I'm gettin' wed to a man 'at either bosses
me about and carries on behind me back or one 'at wants to breed like
a rabbit, they've another think coming.

Marjorie I don't care as I like t'sound o' that.

Bessie I don't care what you like, Marjorie. I'm saying what I think.

Marjorie Eeh, you know, you are like me dad, Bessie. You've allus had
more of him in you than either me or our Carol.

Gladys Thank goodness she's not at home to see all this.

Bessie (*loudly*) I am not like me dad. I wish people 'ud stop saying I'm
like him, because I'm not.

Marjorie There y'are, you're proving it with every word you say.

Gladys You can't stop single all your days, Bessie.

Bessie I can that, an' all me nights an' all.

Gladys Well, I suppose it depends what you want out of a husband.

Bessie Nothing 'at I've seen so far, thank you very much.

Marjorie You'll learn as you get a bit older, Bessie.

Gladys Nay, we've been saying that for years. She'll soon be too late to
learn owt.

Bessie You're the ones 'at's too late, not me.

Gladys Have you been having some trouble wi' Bob, Bessie?

Bessie Aye, I sent him on his way.

Gladys What did you fall out about?

Bessie It started with him not keeping his hands to himself.

Marjorie Is that all? He's only human, isn't he, flesh an' blood? You've
been engaged well over two years now, I don't wonder he's a bit im-
patient. Jim were allus on at me afore we were wed, trying it on. But I

allus used to tell meself 'at I'd be wondering what I wa' marrying if he didn't.

Bessie You found out soon enough, anyway.

Marjorie Our Kevin wa' premature, Bessie. Me mam knows that an' so do you. So what're you drivin' at?

Bessie I'm sayin' 'at *I'm* not gettin' wed to live in a house full of snotty-nosed kids an' wet nappies, wi' out two ha'pennies to rub together. That's what I'm sayin'.

Marjorie No, lass, you live in a bungalow like a furniture-shop window where you can polish your ashtrays all day and have a fit every time some bairn hits a ball into your garden.

Bessie It's everybody to their taste.

Marjorie That's right, love. So why not keep your thoughts about my taste to yourself.

Gladys Will you two stop fratching. Your father 'ull be in afore long and we're still no forrader with what we ought to do.

Bessie Face him with it, that's what I say.

Marjorie I say get to know who she is and where she lives.

Gladys I must say, I'd like to know a bit more.

Bessie If it were a husband o' mine I'd get to know all I needed to know by throwing the flamin' things in his face and seeing what he had to say for himself.

Marjorie Aye, happen so, but you're not me mam, Bessie, so just shurrup a minute while we have a think. What about putting t'kettle on for a cup o' tea, Mother?

Gladys That's not a bad idea.

Gladys gets up and goes into the kitchen. The back door opens and Luther's voice is heard

Luther (*off*) Now then, you've come back then.

Gladys (*off*) Aye, I've come back.

Marjorie Oh, Lord, there's me dad back already.

Luther comes in, followed by Gladys

Luther What's this, then, a meeting o' t'women's union?

Bessie Aye, we thought it wa' time we got organized a bit.

Luther Happen so, happen so. (*He is now quite amiable after his few pints*) If that's a cup o' tea you're makin', Gladys, I'll join you. I don't suppose that comes under t'embargo, eh?

Gladys Go an' mash it if you want some. Put enough tea and water in for four.

Luther Aye, all right.

Luther exits to the kitchen

Gladys Where've you put them things, Marjorie?

Marjorie (*lifting her hand*) They're here.

Gladys You'd best put 'em out o' t'road.
Marjorie 'Ere you take 'em.

Marjorie thrusts the packet at Gladys, who takes it automatically. She suddenly realizes what she is holding

Gladys I don't want 'em. (*She hands the packet to Bessie*)
Bessie What can I do with 'em. (*She passes them back to Marjorie*)
Marjorie I know. (*She looks round. Her eyes light up. She gets up and goes to Luther's suit. She slips the packet into the inside pocket and puts the suit in a conspicuous position over the sofa*)
Gladys (*hissing*) What you done that for?
Marjorie Wait an' see.

Luther comes back in and takes a stance in front of the fire

Luther It'll boil in a minute. Cold out tonight. Did Jack Harper call here earlier on?
Bessie Yes. I told him you were down at *The Greyhound.*
Luther Aye, somebody said he'd been looking for me. I must ha' been in t'club while he were there. (*His eyes fall on the suit*) What's me suit doin' there?
Gladys I asked our Marjorie to pop it in at the cleaners.
Luther I didn't know it wanted cleaning. (*He goes and picks up the suit*)
Gladys I thought it did.
Luther Aye, well, happen so. (*He begins as casually as possible to check the pockets*)
Marjorie You didn't leave any pound notes in, Dad?
Luther That'll be the day. (*His hand in the inside pocket feels the packet. He freezes, not knowing what to think, then removes his hand and lightly brushes it down the jacket*) Aye, well. I'll take it and put it away.

Luther goes out through the hall door

Marjorie looks triumphantly at Gladys and Bessie

Marjorie There, then, what d'you think o' that?
Bessie The old devil! Now are you convinced?
Gladys I suppose I have to be.
Bessie What do we do now?
Marjorie I don't know, but let's not talk in here. (*She nods towards the hall door indicating that they might be overheard*) Is that kettle boiling, Mam?
Gladys I expect so.
Marjorie Right, let's go in there. I can think better over a cup of tea.

Bessie, Marjorie and Gladys exit to the kitchen closing the door behind them, and revealing Bob against the wall

Bob Blimey!

*Bob glances round to see if the coast is clear and is creeping towards the
door when Luther comes back, still dazed and puzzled*

Luther (*startled*) What the hell! (*He sees who it is*) I thought I'd made it
plain that I don't want to see your face in this house again.
Bob But, Luther, I've got something to tell you. I've just heard something
that's very important. Something you ought to know about.
Luther Look, lad, I've got enough problems of me own.
Bob Just give me a couple of words, that's all.
Luther Right. Two words. Bugger off!
Bob (*draws himself up*) If that's the way you want it.

Bob exits through the hall

*Luther walks up and down the room, then takes the packet from his pocket
and looks at it*

Luther I wonder . . . Well, electronically tested or not, if they've been
through the dry cleaners they won't be much use now.

CURTAIN

SCENE 2

The same. Some days later, Saturday morning

*The radio is playing, but the sound can hardly be heard as Gladys is wielding
the vacuum-cleaner. Bessie comes in from the kitchen*

Bessie Mam.

Gladys does not hear. Bessie comes closer

   Mam!
Gladys (*startled*) Ooh! Whatever did you want to do that for? (*She switches
off the cleaner*)
Bessie That's better.

The Radio Voice breaks in

Radio And now after that splendid cup of BBC coffee, today's recipe.
Are you ready? It's stuffed tomatoes . . .

Bessie switches it off

Bessie And that's better still.
Gladys I was miles away.
Bessie I don't suppose me dad's said anything yet?
Gladys. No. Our Marjorie said not to let on 'at we knew anything, so I
haven't. It's a strain, though, Bessie. I don't know 'at I can stand it
much longer.
Bessie Maybe you won't need to. What time did he get in last night?

Gladys Just after midnight. I reckoned to be asleep. I didn't want to talk to him. I don't want to listen to his lies.

Bessie We'll find out a bit more about it, anyway, when our Marjorie comes round. What time did she say?

Gladys She'll have to wait till Jim comes in to see to the bairns. So it'll be twelve or after.

Bessie I'm wondering what she told Jim last night. I said to her, you can't just go out of the house for two or three hours in an evening without a reason, but she said not to worry, she'd think of something.

Gladys You should have gone, Bessie, if anybody had to.

Bessie What d'you mean "if anybody had to"? Somebody had to, hadn't they? You want to know what me dad's up to, don't you?

Gladys Well, of course I do. All t'same . . .

Bessie An' I was working over, wasn't I? Anyway, you couldn't trust me to control me temper.

Gladys She must have told Jim something.

Bessie She'll tell Jim nothing. She knows how to handle him, I'll say that much for her. Anyway, if she's not coming till twelve I'll pop up to the shops for half an hour. I want some cigs.

Gladys I thought you'd stopped smoking.

Bessie So did I.

Gladys Have you seen Bob lately?

Bessie Not since that night.

Gladys Isn't it time you were making a move, then? You'll pass his house on your way to the shops.

Bessie He knows where I am if he wants me.

Gladys He knows where you are, but does he know you want him? An' there's only a chilly welcome here, what with your father an' all.

Bessie If I bump into him in the street I shan't ignore him. But I'm not eating humble pie. I mean to start as we'll go on for all our married life. That is, if we do patch it up.

Gladys You'll find you can't plan that far ahead, lass. An' most men like to feel they've got the last word.

Bessie You're saying that because you've always let me father have his own way.

Gladys I've always let him *think* he was getting his own way. And it's worked very well.

Bessie Up to now.

Gladys Granted. Up to now.

Bessie Mam—do you think this is the first time?

Gladys What? Your father? Well, I suppose so.

Bessie You don't know, though, do you?

Gladys It's never crossed me mind before.

Bessie But it does happen.

Gladys Oh, aye, all the time. But to other folk. Not to you.

Bessie I suppose so . . .

Gladys (*suddenly*) I can't help wondering what she's like.

Bessie You'll know soon enough if our Marjorie's done her detective work properly.

Gladys I only hope he didn't spot her. . . . I feel as if twelve o'clock'll never arrive. It's like waiting to go down for an operation.

The front doorbell rings. Gladys goes into the hall

Carol! Whatever are you doing here?
Carol (*off*) Hello, Mam.

Carol enters, wearing a sweater and jeans and carrying a small duffel bag which she drops on the sofa. She is just twenty-one. Gladys follows her in

I thought I'd come to the front door and give you a surprise. Hello, Bessie.
Bessie Hello, Carol. I didn't think you'd be on holiday for a couple of weeks yet.
Carol I'm not. I just suddenly felt like coming home for the week-end.
Gladys It's good to see you, love. Take your coat off. The kettle's on, it only needs turning up.

Gladys goes into the kitchen

Bessie There's nothing wrong, is there?
Carol (*taking off her coat*) No, why? Should there be?
Bessie It just seems funny for you to be home when you'll be back for Easter in a fortnight.
Carol Well, that's it, really. I've got a chance to go abroad with some friends at Easter and I knew Mam and Dad would be upset if I didn't put in an appearance. So, on the spur of the moment, I thought I'd come now.
Bessie What it must be like to be able to just pick up and go where you please when you please.
Carol You're as free as I am, Bessie.
Bessie I've got a living to earn.
Carol And I've got a degree to get, and before very long now. You can get a job almost anywhere, can't you? You've got nothing to tie you down, except maybe Bob.
Bessie It's how you look at things. You're a lot freer than me in that. I've got a dull old nine-to-five job and I work all day with a lot of other dull old nine-to-fivers.
Carol It'll soon be my turn.
Bessie But you've at least been away for three years and learned to spread your wings. I'm nearly thirty and I don't expect I'll ever even flutter mine now.
Carol Why don't you just up sticks and go off for a holiday? You and Bob?
Bessie We're saving for the house. Or we were.

Gladys enters with the tea things

Gladys What's that?

Bessie Oh, nothing important. I'll be off.

Gladys Aren't you waiting for a cup of tea?

Bessie No, I'll not bother. (*She turns at the door to the hall*) Don't forget our Marjorie's coming.

Gladys I won't.

Bessie goes out

Carol What did she mean about Bob? (*She pours out the tea*)

Gladys Oh, they've had a little tiff, that's all.

Carol I don't know how they go on like they do. They've been going steady ever since I went away to university.

Gladys Well, they're saving to build a house.

Carol And building up a lot of frustration with it.

Gladys I haven't noticed.

Carol Oh, Mam, you know what I mean. Our Bessie's in a terrible rut. She doesn't seem to be able to do anything on impulse any more. I can see what they'll have together—if ever they do get married, that is. A planned kitchen, a planned garden, a planned budget, and a planned family.

Gladys puts her cup down suddenly

What's up, Mam? Is something wrong?

Gladys No, nothing. (*She changes the subject*) How did you get here?

Carol Hitched.

Gladys On your own?

Carol It was broad daylight.

Gladys Not at the time you must have set off.

Carol Well, near enough. I woke up early, thought jigger it, I'll go, packed my little bag, hopped out on the side of the road, and here I am.

Gladys Just like that, eh? Well, I know you think I'm old-fashioned, but life isn't as simple as you make it out to be, for all your education.

Carol And it's not as menacing as you make it out to be. Besides, I can look after myself.

Gladys Let's hope you're right.

Carol What time's she coming round?

Gladys Who?

Carol Marjorie.

Gladys She isn't. Oh, yes, I'd forgotten.

Carol Come on, Mam, what's going on?

Gladys I don't know what you mean.

Carol I know there's something. I could smell it as soon as I walked in. What have you been up to?

Gladys Look, love, your father was out late last night and he's only just getting up.

Carol At the dogs?

Gladys Aye. Now he'll be down any minute. Will you do something for me?

Carol (*deciding to play along*) Go on.

Gladys It's hard to explain, but—(*with a sudden idea*)—I've got a surprise
for him. Something I don't want him to see.

Carol For his birthday?

Gladys Yes. No, that's not till August. No, it's just a surprise.

Carol And what is it?

Gladys It wouldn't be a surprise if I told you.

Carol (*resigned*) Okay. What do you want me to do?

Gladys He'll be going down to the pub like he always does on a Saturday
dinner-time, but I want him out of the house by a quarter to twelve.
If you could manage it—say you'll walk down with him but you've
got to be at the post office by twelve—something like that. You can
manage something, can't you?

Carol And our Marjorie's in on this as well?

Gladys Well, yes. Listen, that's him coming now. Not a word.

Luther enters in his suit but without his shoes

Luther Well now, what's this? Another mouth to feed?

Carol It's a good job I don't take you seriously. (*She goes to Luther and
kisses him*)

Luther (*amiably*) I didn't know Easter fell a fortnight early this year.

Carol I'll begin to think visits are rationed.

Luther You ration 'em, love, not us. How did you get here?

Carol I hitched.

Luther On your own?

Carol Now don't you start! I've already had it out with Mam. Honestly,
you'd think the world was full of people whose sole intention was to
rape young women—in daylight, too!

Gladys Carol, you shouldn't talk like that.

Carol Well, really! Listen, I stood at the roundabout on the A1 for nearly
twenty minutes and none of your wild young men pulled up for me. In
the end I was taken pity on by a kind old lorry driver.

Gladys You can't trust *any*body these days.

Carol He was as safe as me dad.

Gladys That's what I mean.

Carol What?

Gladys (*hastily covering up*) I mean you can't go by appearances. You
never know with people nowadays.

Carol I know a bit about people. I'm studying them, remember?

Luther Aye, you read your sociology at college and think because you
know a few facts and figures you know all. But there's nowt to beat a
bit of experience.

Carol I didn't say that. But you can learn something from facts and figures,
as you call them. And what I've learned is that the world's a better place
for knowing. I can't spend my whole life distrusting strangers and
thinking I'm going to be cheated or seduced by every man that
comes along. You *have* to trust people. And I know I'm young but I do
know quite a lot about them. I talk to them, all the time. You'd be sur-

prised how much they'll tell you about themselves and their private lives.

Luther I wouldn't. I've seen them reports.

Carol You just see the juicy bits that sell the papers.

Gladys Well, I think people ought to keep such things to themselves. It's not normal.

Carol Nobody *knows* what's normal. That's what we're trying to find out. People aren't all the same. And their views about right and wrong are changing.

Gladys They are that! I'll agree with you there.

Carol And when we really get to know more about one another, and we've cleared a lot of that old dead wood away, we might get things like sex into perspective. Devalue it so that it takes its proper place, and we can all worry about more important things.

Luther Like what?

Carol Like hunger and poverty.

Luther I don't think you'll learn your Mam an' me much about them. We've had our share.

Carol Then I'll question you about them and leave your sex life out of it.

Luther Aye, do that. An' I'll tell you summat—for all your brains an' education you're just like other women in one respect.

Carol What's that?

Luther You talk too much.

The conversation has been light-hearted. Luther and Gladys are aware of the generation gap and make allowances for Carol's outlook which they wouldn't for Marjorie or Bessie

Gladys Well, if that settles that I wish you'd all get out of the way and let me get some vegetables on for the dinner. It's getting on for a quarter to twelve and I haven't finished cleaning up.

Carol All right. Are you going down to *The Greyhound,* Dad?

Luther Aye, I'm all but ready now.

Carol Is that a new tie you've got on?

Luther This? Oh aye, aye. I saw it in a shop window in Calderford t'other Saturday. Took a fancy to it.

Carol Very smart. You'd better watch him, Mam. I haven't seen him in a new tie for years.

Gladys It takes people in funny ways.

Luther Eh?

Gladys Spring. Your shoes are by the hearth when you want 'em. I've given 'em a rub over.

Luther Eh? What? Have you?

Gladys Aye. You don't want mucky shoes when you've got a new tie on, do you?

Luther (*puzzled*) No. No, I suppose you don't. (*He puts his shoes on*)

Gladys I don't like to see a man become careless with his appearance as he gets on a bit. When he dresses well it shows he's still got an interest in life.

Luther I suppose you're right.

Carol Are you going to the match this afternoon?
Luther Aye.
Gladys Will you be out late?
Luther No, I think I'll get to bed early.
Gladys Happen you're a bit tired. Too many late nights are no good for
   you at your age.
Luther I don't know why you keep harping on about age, woman. You
   put years on me.
Carol Here's your coat.
Luther Are you trying to get rid of me?
Carol No, just being a dutiful daughter.

Luther puts his coat on and goes to the kitchen door, where he turns

Luther I'm not saying I'm in favour of all this prying into folks' private
   affairs, but I wouldn't mind reading one o' them reports. It might be
   interesting.
Carol You'd be surprised.
Luther Aye. Mind you I reckon you'd have to take it with a pinch of salt.
   I bet there's a bit o' braggin' goes on.

Bob and Bessie come through the kitchen behind Luther

Carol Oh, hello, Bob.
Bob Hello, Carol. Nice to see you. I'm sorry, Luther, I thought you'd be
   out by now.

*Luther stares at Bob as if he will say something. Then he turns and crosses,
going out through the hall*

Gladys Is that silly daft behaviour still going on?
Bob Aye. I'm beginning to feel like the invisible man.
Carol What's it all about?
Gladys It's a union job. Your dad's not speaking to Bob, and neither is
   anybody else at work.
Carol You mean you're in Coventry? But that's terrible.
Bob Oh, it's funny how soon you get used to it. You begin to live inside
   your own head. It's not as if most people had much to say worth listening
   to, is it?
Gladys Carol, I thought you were going to walk down with your father.
Carol But he's gone anyway, now.
Gladys That's not the point. Is it?
Carol Oh, you mean you want *me* out of the way as well? If you can wait
   till I run a comb through my hair.
Bob Can anybody join in, or is it a secret?
Bessie Mind your own business, Bob Carter.
Gladys I didn't know Bessie had gone out to meet you, Bob.
Bessie I didn't, I went for some cigs.
Bob I bumped into her at the corner, so I thought I'd walk back with her.
Bessie Nobody asked you to.

Gladys Why don't you two stop fratching?

Bob Nay, you'll have to ask Bessie that.

Gladys She's talking to you, isn't she?

Bob She wasn't on the way up here. (*He goes into a music-hall routine*) "I say, I say, my girl friend hasn't talked to me for seven days." "You're lucky, my wife hasn't stopped for seven years."

Carol laughs

Bessie Ha, ha, ha.

Bob Well, it's a reaction, at least.

Gladys (*anxiously*) Bessie, it's nearly twelve o'clock. Wouldn't you like to walk Bob back home?

Bob I'm in no hurry.

Gladys Our Marjorie's coming round, you see, Bob. You won't want to listen to a lot of women nattering away.

Bob (*sitting on the sofa*) I don't mind. It'll make a change to hear people talking.

Gladys But, Bob . . .

Bessie Can't you take a hint?

Bob Oh, you don't *want* me to stay?

Carol It's all right, Bob. They don't want me either. I'm going down to the post office. Why don't you walk down with me and I'll give you the privilege of buying me a coffee.

Bob (*brightly*) Yes, I think I'd like that. Shall I see you tonight, Bessie? Usual time?

Bessie I don't know.

Bob Well, I'll be there anyway.

Gladys I'm right glad you're home, love. (*She kisses Carol impetuously*)

Carol But you want to get rid of me. (*Cheerfully*) Okay. Come on, Bob.

Bob See you later, Bessie.

Bessie Happen so.

Bob and Carol go out through the hall

Gladys Well! I thought that was going to be awkward.

Bessie Our Carol would just walk in like that.

Gladys Nay, Bessie, we're always glad to see her. The thing is, how are we going to stop her from finding out? She knows already that something's up.

Bessie We'll cross that bridge when we hear what our Marjorie's got to tell us.

Gladys Aye . . . (*Pauses for a moment, then begins to clear the vacuum-cleaner away*)

Bessie takes the tea-things into the kitchen. Marjorie comes in through the kitchen as Bessie comes back

Gladys You're here, Marjorie. You've timed it well.

Marjorie Almost too well. I bobbed into the entry as they came out of

the front door. What's our Carol doing at home? Does she know about
it?

Gladys That she doesn't. And I don't want her to. It's bad enough you
two knowing.

Bessie Well, come on, Marjorie. Tell us the worst.

Gladys Bessie!

Marjorie It all went like clockwork.

Gladys You're sure he didn't see you? I shouldn't want him to think we
were spying on him.

Bessie Talk sense, Mam. After what he's been doing to you? Start at the
beginning, Marjorie.

Marjorie Well, I got on the bus.

Bessie The half past seven?

Marjorie Aye, that's right.

Gladys That's the one he always catches.

Marjorie I knew he'd be upstairs where he could have a smoke, so I
waited at the next stop, in the shelter, and when the bus came I nipped
on smartish and went right up to the front, downstairs. I was wondering
how I could get off without him seeing me, but as luck would have it,
he went all the way to the terminus and I waited for a minute before I
went after him.

Gladys Where did he go then?

Marjorie He went up King Street. At first I thought he was going to the
dogs.

Bessie He's going to the dogs, all right.

Gladys Bessie . . .

Marjorie But he went into the first pub. You know, the one they did up
posh just before Christmas.

Bessie *The Crown*, you mean.

Marjorie Aye, that's the one.

Gladys I'll crown him.

Marjorie Anyway, I couldn't see through the window and I daren't go in
for fear of coming face to face with him, so I just waited on the other
side of the road. Then it started raining. I was wet through by the time
he came out. Soaked.

Bessie Never mind, Marjorie, it's all in a good cause.

Gladys Had he got somebody with him.

Marjorie Aye, and he was laughing.

Gladys I'm not sure I'd've owned that. I haven't heard him laugh in years.

Marjorie Oh, he laughed, all right. Like he'd just heard the best joke in the
world.

Bessie Well, it might be a joke to him. But, by God . . .

Gladys Did you see what she was like? Was she a fast-looking piece?

Marjorie Well, no, not exactly. A bit flashy, maybe. But well set up an'
smartly dressed. It was the way she hung on to his arm 'at got me. Just
as if she owned him. An' lookin' up into his face all the time.

Bessie Just the sort to suck up to him an' make him think he's a big man.

Gladys He allus did like lasses to suck up to him, as a lad. But I thought
he'd grown out of all that donkeys' years ago.

Bessie They never grow out of it.

Gladys I wouldn't have classed all men alike before. But now . . .

Marjorie But now we know.

Bessie Aye, now we know.

Gladys Go on, then, Marjorie. Get on with your tale.

Marjorie It was coming down cats and dogs by this time. She had an umbrella but all I'd got was that blue raincoat of mine on. I never bothered to have it reproofed the last time it was cleaned and it lets the water straight through. I tell you I'm surprised I haven't gone down with pneumonia. I was soaked through.

Gladys Marjorie . . .

Marjorie I'm coming to it. They went round a corner and got into a red car. Took me by surprise, that did. I had to nip into a yard or else I'd have been caught in the headlights.

Bessie They drove off, did they?

Marjorie Aye, up the moor road.

Gladys The moor road?

Bessie It's just like the *News of the World*.

Gladys You don't think they—(*she can't bring herself to say it*)—in the car?

Marjorie What? Oh no, I shouldn't think so. It was only a mini. I'd ha' thought me dad was past that sort o' thing.

Gladys There's a lot we thought he was past.

Bessie So that's all you found out?

Marjorie Oh, no. No, I had a brainwave. I went back and into the pub.

Gladys On your own?

Marjorie Well, I thought if she can wait for me dad in the pub on her own what am I worried about.

Gladys You should have come home then when you were so wet through, and let me have it out straight with him.

Marjorie Nay, I wasn't going to give up so easy. It's a lovely pub now, though Bessie. You want to get Bob to take you sometime. A lovely thick carpet and nice soft pink lights. I thought what can I order to warm me up a bit, so I had a sherry. I knew you'd make it right with me.

Bessie You what?

Marjorie Over me expenses. There was seventeen pence bus fare and fifteen pence for the sherry.

Bessie Why didn't you have a double brandy while you were at it?

Gladys Thirty-two pence I owe you. Remind me.

Bessie (*opening her purse; coldly*) Here—there's thirty-five.

Marjorie It's all right for you, Bessie, earning a wage and only yourself to keep. Thirty-two pence makes a big hole in my housekeeping.

Bessie Well, now you're three pence to t'good.

Gladys How you two can fratch over a few shillings when all this is going on . . . Did you find anything else out, Marjorie, or are you just talking for the sake of it?

Marjorie I like that! Who was it who trailed all that way after him and risked getting her death o' cold standing in the pelting rain?

Bessie It was you, Marjorie, love, and we're very grateful to you.

Marjorie All right, then. Where had I got to?

Bessie You were in the pub, wet through, and drinking sherry on expenses.

Gladys Bessie! Just go on with it, will you, Marjorie.

Marjorie Well, I got talking to the landlord and reckoned I was waiting for a friend but I was a bit late and I might have missed her. She might have been with an elderly man in a brown overcoat, I said. "Oh," he says, "you mean the lady with the red mini. They're two of my Friday night regulars. I've known her for ages. She works at Burnetts. I only know that, though," he says, "because she fitted my wife one." Well, I'm nodding as though I know all about it already, but I draw him out a bit more and it turns out her name's Fairchild and she's a corset fitter for Burnetts.

Gladys Did he say how long they'd been going into the pub together?

Marjorie Aye, the best part of a year.

Bessie A year! The old devil!

Gladys I blame meself in one way, for not smelling something was wrong before this.

Bessie You can't blame yourself, Mam. He's been cunning. All his big talk about principles. I reckon he leaves them at work in his overall pocket.

Gladys It might have been better if he'd left them things there an' all.

Majorie Nay, Mam!

Gladys Well, what's to do now? I'm hardly t'sort to go into *The Crown* an' face 'em out.

Marjorie You won't have to. I've seen to that.

Gladys Oh, how?

Marjorie I thought it'd be a good idea for all of us to have a look at her close to. Weigh her up properly and then see what's to be done.

Gladys Look at her? How are we going to do that? And what do you mean "all of us"?

Marjorie What I say. We know where she works, don't we?

Gladys An' what do you expect me to do, Marjorie? Go an' pull her hair out for her in Burnetts' underwear department?

Marjorie No, Mam. We get her here.

Bessie Here?

Gladys What d'you mean "here"?

Marjorie Here—in this room. In fact, it's all arranged. I rang her from the 'phone-box this morning. "One of my friends recommended you," I said. "I need a fitting. You do do fittings in customers' own homes?" "If our customers wish it, modom," she says—very posh, she is, on the phone—"that's part of our service."

Gladys But you don't need a corset.

Marjorie As a matter of fact I could do with one. But I shan't get one. I've all on to afford a new pair of pants from Marks and Sparks. Anyway, she doesn't know that, does she?

Bessie An' when have you fixed this for, Marjorie?

Marjorie Seven o'clock on Monday night. I knew me dad always goes out to a meeting on Mondays.

Gladys But why bring her here?

Marjorie It's no good at my place, with all the kids, is it? Don't worry, I didn't give her your address, in case she knew where me dad lives. And I gave her my married name. I said it was a bit tricky to find so I'd meet her at the post office and show her the way.

Bessie You're sure you've got the right woman?

Marjorie Oh, yes. Mrs Fairchild, and she'll be in a red mini.

Gladys Mrs?

Marjorie She must be a widow.

Bessie Divorced, more like.

Gladys I don't like this. I wish we'd never started it.

Bessie You didn't start it. He did.

Marjorie But we'll finish it.

Gladys Nay, we shouldn't be doing this.

Marjorie You're not turning soft, are you, Mam?

Bessie You can't let 'em get away with it.

Gladys I don't think this is the way.

Marjorie It's either find some way of warning her off, or face me dad with it, fair and square.

Bessie And what's to stop him doing as he likes afterwards then?

Marjorie Aye, you can't lock him in the house every night.

Gladys Nay, if he knew I'd found out . . .

Bessie What?

Gladys Well, he'd—surely . . .

Bessie ⎫
Marjorie ⎬ Mam . . .

Gladys Well, happen you're right.

Marjorie I shall have to get back. I've got nowt done at home with all this. And I think I've a cold coming on. Monday night, now. Don't forget.

Gladys I'm hardly likely to forget.

Marjorie (*at the door*) No, well . . . Oh, and by the way. You don't think he tumbled to anything after we'd put them things back in his pocket, do you?

Gladys I don't think so.

Bessie Did you have another look?

Gladys Aye, the next day. They were gone.

Marjorie He'd put 'em somewhere else, d'you think?

Gladys Well, I wondered. So I did something I've never done in all me married life before. I went through his wallet.

Bessie And?

Gladys (*nodding*) But there weren't two any more. There were three.

Majorie The old devil must ha' bought another packet!

Bessie He's a flamin' sex maniac!

Gladys Now, Bessie.

Bessie Well, it's not—it's not decent in a man of his age. It wouldn't be decent anyway—and not with a corset fitter from Burnetts.

Marjorie I don't know about you, Bessie, but I can hardly wait for Monday night . . .

Bessie Me neither.

Marjorie Just fancy—if she'd been on the Pill we might never have known!

Gladys looks from one to the other, with some apprehension, as the Lights fade and—

the CURTAIN *falls*

ACT II

Scene 1

The same. Monday evening, approaching seven o'clock

Gladys is plumping cushions as Bessie comes in

Bessie Give over, Mam.

Gladys Give over what?

Bessie You must have been rushing about dusting and cleaning all day. Anybody 'ud think we'd got the Queen coming for supper.

Gladys I'd feel a lot easier if we had.

Bessie Just sit down and take it easy. Has our Carol gone out yet?

Gladys She'll be gone in a minute. She's off to the pictures.

Bessie I've never seen the place so tidy. You've no need to work your blood to water for the likes of her.

Gladys No, but I'll feel easier in me own mind. I don't like the idea of her coming here at all, but at least I'll give her nothing to criticize.

Bessie She won't notice. We'll be looking at *her*, remember. She won't have a clue who you are.

Gladys I just don't know how I'll ever keep it up.

Bessie All you've got to do is remember that as long as she doesn't know who you are you've got the advantage.

Gladys If you ask me, all the advantage is with her.

Bessie For the time being, maybe.

Gladys She's free, she's younger than me—or I suppose she is—and she has all the fun. D'you know what's hurt most of all I've heard since our Marjorie took his suit to the cleaners?

Bessie What?

Gladys Her telling us about the two of 'em coming out of that pub, laughing. Aye, laughing! Over and over I've asked meself—what's he got to laugh about? He used to laugh when I first knew him, but that's a long time ago. She must be summat special to be able to make him let himself go like that, whatever our Marjorie made of her.

Bessie It's obvious what sort of woman she is.

Gladys I'm not so sure. He's never been interested in women before. I'm positive.

Bessie Well, he married you.

Gladys Aye, but he's never bothered me overmuch.

Bessie Come off it, Mam. You've got three daughters. You didn't get us with Green Shield stamps.

Gladys I'd never have expected it of him. He was never that keen.

Bessie I don't know what comes over men when they get to middle-age. You'd think they'd cool down, but no, they seem to get worked-up more

easily than ever. Then some of 'em go funny, like that chap who . . .
(*She stops having blurted out too much*)

Gladys Which chap?

Bessie Oh, it was nothing.

Gladys Is it summat you've never told me?

Bessie Oh, it was a long time ago.

Gladys What was a long time ago?

Bessie Well, it was when I first started at Mertons and I was going to
work on the train. He used to get on at night and sit in a corner, reading
his paper. About fifty, he was, with glasses. He looked harmless enough.
Anyway, one night I glanced across and he was—well, you know,
showing himself.

Gladys How d'you mean?

Bessie You know—exposing.

Gladys Never! Whatever did you do?

Bessie I didn't know what to do. I thought, I won't make a fuss because
that's what he wants. So I pretended I hadn't noticed. Anyhow, he got
out at the next station.

Gladys Well, you've kept that to yourself.

Bessie Oh, I told our Marjorie, but I was too embarrassed somehow to
mention it to you.

Gladys Did you never see him again?

Bessie Aye, once. Just before Christmas, it was. He smiled at me but I
took no notice and got on with me book. Then a bit later I realized that
everybody else had got out and there was only the two of us left in the
carriage. And he did it again. Like before.

Gladys Good heavens! What did you do that time?

Bessie Well, I'd done some shopping in the dinner-hour and I suddenly
remembered I'd bought one of them aerosol sprays full of gold paint,
for the Christmas decorations.

Gladys Yes, I remember you bringing that home.

Bessie Well, I got it out, took the cap off, and . . .

Gladys You mean . . . ?

Bessie Aye, I got a direct hit. He never caught my train again.

Gladys I'll bet his face was a picture.

Bessie Aye. That's not all.

They laugh, then Gladys suddenly becomes serious

Gladys It's not really funny, though.

Bessie Our Marjorie thought it was. She couldn't stop laughing when I
told her. Anyway, they always say that sort aren't dangerous.

Gladys They're upsetting, though. Fancy sitting, minding your own business, in a train and . . . (*She listens*) Is that them at the front door?

Bessie No.

Gladys I thought I heard a noise. I wish they'd come, if they're coming.
Let's get it over.

Bessie They'll be here before long. Stop worrying.

The doorbell sounds

Now just sit back and look relaxed. I'll go. No, not as if you're going to take off and run a mile. Relax or she'll guess something's up.

Gladys tries to look comfortable

Bessie goes out to the front door. There are indistinct voices, then she comes back with Bob

Bob Hello, Mrs Stringer.
Gladys Oh, it's you.
Bob Aye, only me. You didn't come Saturday night, Bessie.
Bessie No, I didn't feel like it.
Bob Oh.
Bessie And I can't come out tonight. I'm busy.
Bob Oh, that's all right.
Bessie In fact, it's not very convenient you being here. We're expecting a visitor.
Bob I'm not stopping. It's just that Carol said she might come with me.
Bessie Carol? Where to?
Bob There's a good picture on at the ABC. We were talking about it on Saturday.
Bessie Saturday?
Bob You know, when you didn't come. I bumped into her later. You don't mind, do you?
Bessie (*who does*) Mind? Why should *I* mind?

Carol comes downstairs. She's wearing a dress instead of the scruffy jeans and sweater she wore previously

(*Accusingly*) You didn't say you were going to the pictures.
Carol I told Mam.
Bessie With Bob, I mean.
Carol It's not definite. Bob said he'd like to see the film and I said I'd go with him if you didn't want to. It's up to you. I don't have to go.
Bessie I can't go. I'm stopping in tonight.
Carol I'll stay in if Mam wants a bit of company.
Bessie (*hastily*) No, you go. I don't like the pictures much, anyway.
Carol They say it's very good.

Bessie turns away

Bob Well, if that's all settled . . . Are you ready, Carol?
Carol Yes.

Bob helps Carol on with her coat, an action which Bessie does not miss

See you later!
Bob Aye, see you later.

Bob and Carol exit cheerfully

Gladys (*after a silence*) You'd best be making your mind up about that young man, Bessie.

Bessie There's plenty of pebbles on the beach.

Gladys But not so many gold nuggets. Bob's all right, if you want my opinion.

Bessie It's no good, Mam. This business of me dad has made me even less inclined to rush into marriage.

Gladys You've been engaged for nigh on three year. That's hardly breaking your neck.

Bessie I'm *not* engaged any more, remember.

Gladys Aye, well. In that case, I reckon Bob can do what he likes.

Gladys suddenly freezes as the doorbell rings

Bessie (*in a loud whisper*) Now, Mam, remember what I said. Relax and act natural. Everything's on our side. She'll know nothing till we're ready to spring it on her.

Gladys (*in a loud whisper*) What d'you mean "spring it on her"? Nobody said anything about . . .

Bessie (*finger to lips*) Sssh!

Bessie goes into the hall and opens the front door. Gladys looks as if she wishes she could hide. She jumps up, takes a quick look at herself in the mirror, pats her hair, and sits down again a split second before Bessie comes in followed by Marjorie and Ann Fairchild. Mrs Fairchild is a handsome woman in her middle-forties, well-groomed and smartly dressed. Her manner is one of a pleasant confidence, her patter smooth and impersonal, keeping a distance between herself and her clients. She shows no curiosity about her surroundings. There is a slight split between herself as a woman and her professional persona, which she picks up and assumes in a rather affected way which, in any other cirumstances, would make Marjorie want to giggle

Marjorie Here we are at last, then, Mother. This is Mrs Fairchild.

Ann Good evening.

Marjorie And my sister. (*After a fractional pause*) Elizabeth.

Bessie is momentarily taken aback by this rare use of her proper name. She nods. She it is who now finds it impossible to relax. The tension of having her father's mistress in the room keeps her wound up, restless, unable to indulge her feelings except in an occasional bitchy remark

Bessie I'll make the tea.

Bessie exits to the kitchen

Ann I'm very sorry to be late. I got held up at the shop, and I knew Mrs Mather was waiting on the street.

Marjorie Oh, I'm getting accustomed to hanging about on street corners.

A look from Gladys

The children, y'know. They've no idea of time.

Gladys You have no children yourself, Mrs Fairchild?

Ann No . . . (*Why should she assume that? For the first time there is just a hint to Ann that all is not as it appears*) No, I'm afraid not.

Marjorie I hope the arrangements for tonight don't seem funny to you, Mrs Fairchild. I mean, meeting on a corner then coming here instead of to me own house. Like a sinister plot.

Again Marjorie is sailing too close to the wind for Gladys who shuts her eyes for a second before chipping in

Gladys Oh, I expect Mrs Fairchild gets to funnier quarters than this on her travels.

Ann Yes, indeed. I've come to expect almost anything. Some women find buying a foundation a most intimate matter.

Marjorie Oh, if we hadn't thought it was an intimate matter we shouldn't have dragged you out all this way.

Gladys Let me take your coat.

Ann Thank you. (*She takes off her coat to reveal a neat dress*)

Marjorie It's a secret, y'see.

Ann Oh?

Marjorie From my husband.

Ann I see.

Bessie enters

Marjorie Married people sometimes have to deceive each other a bit, don't you think so?

Ann It depends, I should think.

Marjorie I don't mean about anything *serious*! But I want this to be a surprise for my Jim.

Bessie What she means is her Jim wouldn't understand her spending money on a corset even though it was making herself look smarter for his sake.

Ann (*eagerly*) Yes, it is a pity, you know, that we can't educate more men to realize what a valuable morale-booster a good, properly fitted corset can be to a woman.

Bessie goes out again

Gladys I expect you don't have any trouble with your own husband on that score?

Ann I'm a widow.

Gladys Oh? And you've not thought about getting married again?

Ann Thinking about it and doing it are two different things. Men aren't all that easy to come by, are they?

Gladys Not unless you're not very particular.

Ann And I'm afraid I must be.

Bessie reappears with the tea-tray

Bessie Then again, there's no accounting for other people's tastes, is there?

Ann That's true.

Gladys You'll have a cup of tea?

Ann It will be very welcome. When I have an evening call I don't eat till late.

Gladys Do you work in the evenings a lot?

Ann It varies.

Bessie It'll upset your social life, I expect.

Ann It does lead to difficulties sometimes. But one's livelihood must come first, mustn't it?

Gladys Oh, yes.

Marjorie Especially with a woman on her own.

Ann Yes. Did you have anything particular in mind, Mrs Mather?

Marjorie What? Oh, for a foundation, you mean.

Ann Have you a special problem, like bosom control, midriff bulge, too full development in the hips or buttocks?

Marjorie (*seriously*) Sad flesh is my main problem.

Ann Oh?

Marjorie My husband always used to say I'd got lovely springy flesh when I first married him. But I lost that when I had my family. Now when he touches me his finger-marks seem to linger for ages, like when you squeeze a lump of putty.

Gladys I've never heard you mention that before, Marjorie.

Marjorie It's true, though.

Ann I'm afraid a foundation won't exactly cure that.

Marjorie (*sadly*) No.

Ann Nevertheless, the right type can work wonders in small ways. A little support and separation here, a little smoothing out and shaping there. And one's clothes look so much better on one.

Bessie Your frock fits beautifully, Mrs Fairchild. Do you wear a foundation?

Ann A one-piece lightweight, yes.

Bessie I thought your figure couldn't be all your own at your age.

Ann No. I am quite proud of what nature and will-power have managed on their own. But *anno Domini* catches up with all of us, and a little assistance is a great help. Perhaps I can show you a few things from the range we handle. (*She gets her case and takes out several foundations*) Something like this, perhaps. It comes in several colours—oyster, flesh pink and black.

Marjorie It's a bit on the heavy side, isn't it? I don't want trussing up like a chicken.

Ann Oh, you'd find perfect freedom of movement. But perhaps this . . .

Marjorie (*winking at Gladys*) I don't think so, do you, Mother?

Ann Well, I agree that you don't seem to need a lot of support. Just something to hold you naturally.

Marjorie You couldn't show me yours, could you?

Ann It may not be just what you . . .

Marjorie Oh, but it's so much better to see one actually worn.

Gladys If you'd like us to leave you, Mrs Fairchild . . .

Ann Oh, there's no need for that. I have modelled foundations.

Bessie In front of mixed audiences?

Ann Occasionally. Professionally mixed. Most laymen seem to be em-
: barrassed by such occasions. As if a woman in a corset weren't more
covered than in most modern swimsuits.

Bessie Shall I help you with your zip?

Ann Oh—well, all right. (*She takes off her frock*)

Bessie Here, I'll hold that for you.

Marjorie It's a lovely frock, isn't it, Bessie?

Bessie Lovely.

During the following speech, Bessie slips out of the room with Ann's dress

Ann (*looking down at herself in her slip*) Now this is rather an expensive
model, but of course I can buy at a discount. (*She lifts the hem of her
slip*) Would you like me to . . . ?

Marjorie If you wouldn't mind. Then we can see it properly.

Ann has got the slip half up when Carol comes in through the kitchen

Carol Hello. We're back earlier than we thought. Oh! I'm sorry.

Marjorie I thought you'd be out for hours yet.

Bob comes in and Ann picks up her coat and holds it in front of her

Carol There was a queue a mile long. Imagine!

Bob So we just came straight back. Sorry if we've interrupted.

Marjorie No, no. Only, I was planning a surprise for Jim. Mrs Fairchild's
measuring me for a corset.

Bob It looks as if you're measuring her.

Carol We're obviously in the way. We'll go and get a cup of coffee for
half an hour.

Gladys Aye, that's right. Mrs Fairchild won't be long now.

Carol goes off through the kitchen

Bob It's like a rehearsal for a French farce. (*He laughs but nobody else
joins in*) Well, good night, Mrs Stringer. We'd best be going.

Bob exits through the kitchen

Ann Stringer? (*Nervously*) That's not a very common name.

Gladys Not till you started making it so.

Marjorie (*warningly*) Mam . . .

Gladys Nay, Marjorie, it's too late for that now. I'm Gladys Stringer to
me friends. Not that I count you among them.

Ann I see. So all this was planned.

Gladys Is that all you've got to say?

Ann (*on her dignity now*) If it was necessary to lure me here by such a
mean and deceitful trick why didn't you say who you were before?

Marjorie Mean and deceitful! You've some room to talk!

Gladys We wanted to have a good look at you.

Majorie Aye, see what sort of a woman me dad was jeopardizing his marriage for. And to tell you to keep away from him.

Ann I should think he's got a say in that matter.

Gladys Why him?

Ann What do you mean?

Gladys I know men can't be all that easily come by for a woman of your age, but you're presentable enough even if you are rotten underneath all your make-up and fine feathers. Couldn't you have found somebody better than him?

Ann If that's all you think of Luther no wonder he went looking else-where.

Gladys You haven't answered my question.

Ann Because he's a man of considerable charm, character and prin-ciple.

Gladys Principle!

Ann And he's good company.

Marjorie He's as miserable as a wet Monday.

Ann To you, perhaps. But not to me.

Marjorie Well, miserable or not, he's not seeing you again, madam.

Ann Has he said so?

Marjorie We've said so.

Ann I'll wait to hear it from him. And I don't see why I should discuss the matter with you. If anybody, it's between your mother and me. Now, if I can have my dress I'll leave you.

Marjorie You'll go nowhere till you promise to leave him alone.

Ann I've already told you I won't.

Marjorie Perhaps if I black your eyes you'll think again.

Gladys Leave it be, Marjorie. Let her go. It's gone far enough.

Marjorie Not for me, it hasn't.

Bessie appears in the doorway with Ann's dress

Ann My dress, if you please.

Bessie You'll get no dress from me. (*She throws the dress along the hall*)

Marjorie (*grabbing at Ann's coat as Ann starts to put it on*) You can go home undressed like the tart you are. (*She pushes her*) Get off, out with you!

Gladys Marjorie, please!

Marjorie Come on.

Marjorie and Bessie push and man-handle Ann across the room and into the hall. In a moment Marjorie returns, picks up Ann's case of samples and handbag and takes them out. The front door slams. Marjorie returns

Gladys You shouldn't have done that, Marjorie. You'll only make it worse, and fill the neighbour's mouths.

Marjorie Let 'em see. It'll happen shame him into doing right.
Gladys Go and give her her dress and coat.
Marjorie I won't.

The door from the kitchen opens and Luther walks in

Luther You won't what? What are you shouting about?
Marjorie You might well ask.
Luther Well, Mother?
Gladys (*with spite*) I'm not your mother. I'm your wife, if you did but
remember.
Luther What's got into everybody?
Gladys (*picking up Ann's coat*) Does this mean anything to you?
Luther Have you had a visitor?
Marjorie You could say that.
Luther I wouldn't have thought it.
Marjorie Oh, don't let us spoil your little dream of love. She didn't call
on us, we asked her here.
Luther So you *did* know. What's her coat doing here now?
Gladys She left it behind.
Luther Left it?

Bessie comes in with Ann's dress

Bessie Hello, Father. She left this as well.
Luther Her frock? What the hell's been going on here. (*To Marjorie*)
What devilment have you been up to?
Bessie I was going to give it to her but happen you'd better take it. (*She
splits a seam with a pair of scissors and rips the dress apart*)
Luther You little bitch! What the hell has it got to do with you? What
sort of family have I raised? My God, that Bob you're going to marry,
I feel bloody sorry for him, gormless bugger though he is.
Gladys (*hopeless in this storm*) You shouldn't have done that, Bessie.
Luther No, Bessie, you bloody shouldn't. But don't bother. I'll make
sure you don't get a chance to humiliate her again. (*To Gladys*) Where is
she now?
Gladys On the front doorstep.
Luther On the doorstep! Without . . . ?
Marjorie Aye. You needn't be bashful. She's been seen in her under-
clothes before. She'd be stark naked if I had my way.

Luther moves to the door

Don't you try to let her in.
Luther (*grimly*) I won't, don't you fret. I'll see she goes. And I'm going
with her.

Luther goes off, taking Ann's coat and dress with him

Marjorie and Bessie look at each other in triumph

Bessie Well then—that's shown them!

Gladys Oh, Marjorie, Bessie, you shouldn't have done it!

CURTAIN

SCENE 2

The same. A few days later, early evening

Gladys and Carol are sitting over tea at the table. There is a silence for some moments after the Curtain rises. They are both absorbed in their thoughts, not saying much

Gladys (*hand on the teapot*) Do you want your cup filling?

Carol No, thanks.

Gladys I'll clear away, then.

Carol What about, Bessie?

Gladys She's stopping behind a while, so she'll have had something at work.

Carol You stay where you are then. I'll do it. (*She goes and gets a tray from the kitchen and puts tea-things on it*)

Gladys Aren't you going back to college at all before Easter?

Carol I might go back for a day or two to pick up some things and see about my holiday arrangements.

Gladys All these days away from your studies, wasted.

Carol Oh, Mum, I couldn't have gone back and concentrated on work, with all—all this going on. I wanted to see something settled.

Gladys Well, isn't it?

Carol You know very well it isn't. There hasn't been a sensible word said in all of it. Just shouting and injured pride, and everybody licking their wounds.

Gladys And what would you like to see?

Carol I'd like to see a bit of quiet discussion, without tempers flaring and everybody getting on their high horse.

Gladys I should have thought I could be excused a bit of injured pride and getting on my high horse.

Carol That's natural. But it won't solve anything, will it? Who do you think you're punishing—him, or yourself? I mean, presumably he wanted that woman, and now he's gone off with her. After what happened here that night he'd no option, had he?

Gladys It wasn't me who got her to come here, nor pushed her out on to the doorstep.

Carol No, it wasn't. So why don't you stop talking like Bessie and Marjorie and speak for yourself.

Gladys What am I supposed to say?

Carol Do you want him to come back?

Gladys He wanted somebody else and now he's gone off with her, so why should he come back?

Carol Because I've asked him to.

Gladys You what?

Carol I've asked him to come and have a talk about it, anyway.

Gladys And when did all this happen?

Carol Last night.

Gladys You saw your father last night? How did you find out where he was?

Carol I phoned Mrs Fairchild at the shop.

Gladys It sounds very easy does that. "I phoned Mrs Fairchild at the shop."

Carol What do you want me to say?

Gladys She's the woman he's living with. You make her sound like a friend.

Carol (*patiently*) I phoned her and she told me that she'd arrange for him to meet me.

Gladys Very kind of her.

Carol And I did. In the station buffet.

Gladys Was she with him?

Carol No.

Gladys And what had he to say for himself?

Carol Hardly anything.

Gladys Well, that's a novelty.

Carol I think he was embarrassed by having to discuss it with me.

Gladys So he's not completely beyond redemption.

Carol Mother, it's no use his coming if you're not going to talk to each other like two civilized human beings.

Gladys Did he say he'd come?

Carol Well, no—not exactly. He said he'd think about it.

Gladys I'll expect him when I see him, then. And I'll decide what I'm going to say to him at the same time.

There is a knock at the back door and Bob's voice is heard

Bob (*off*) Hello! Can I come in?

Gladys Who's this?

Carol It sounds like Bob.

Bob appears in the kitchen doorway

Bob Hello, Mrs Stringer, Carol. I hope I'm not interrupting anything.

Gladys You're in now, whether you are or not. Our Bessie's working over.

Bob I know. I wondered if you'd heard the news about Croslands.

Gladys What news is that?

Bob They're talking about laying a hundred and fifty men off. Transferring one whole process to Northumberland. They've called the union in to discuss redundancy.

Carol Does it affect you, Bob?

Bob Oh, aye. And your dad. We'll both be out of work before long.

Gladys So he's out of a job as well. How are the mighty fallen. I'll be back in a while, I'm going round to our Marjorie's.

Carol What if my dad arrives?

Gladys He'll have to wait that's all. I expect he has to hang about for his fancy piece sometimes so he'll be used to it.

Carol Mother . . .

But Gladys has gone

Bob Has anybody seen him since he left?

Carol I did, last night.

Bob Would he talk to you?

Carol He didn't say much. Did Bessie tell you what happened?

Bob Aye, with full details. Her and Marjorie—by crikey, if they could have done it they'd have flogged that woman naked through t'village.

Carol All outraged virtue.

Bob All getting their own back for years of your dad's domineering. Don't think I don't know. Your Bessie worked herself up so much, telling me about it, I thought she was gonna have an orgasm—I'm sorry, I shouldn't have said that.

Carol (*with a shrug*) We're both grown-up people, and friends.

Bob Friends, aye. I suppose you and your friends at college say pretty much what you like to one another.

Carol Well, we try to have honest discussions without keeping half the facts under the carpet.

Bob Aye, well I popped in for a couple of glasses of beer after work. I don't usually drink so early and on an empty stomach, but I wanted me tongue loosening a bit.

Carol Oh?

Bob I suppose you'll have to be getting back to college any day?

Carol I suppose I shall, or they'll end the term without me.

Bob I've enjoyed having you at home. We've never seen so much of each other, or talked so much before.

Carol No, we haven't. I've enjoyed it as well.

Bob What it must be to have a real education, though. I mean, I read quite a lot, and I know some words 'at you don't hear said very often.

Carol (*smiling*) I've noticed.

Bob It's having somebody to use 'em on, though. Being able to sharpen your mind on other people's. That's what I call education.

Carol What did you mean about Bessie, Bob? Do you mean she's cold.

Bob Cold, set in her ways, without imagination, that's Bessie.

Carol And you couldn't have said to her what you just said to me? About having an orgasm.

Bob She'd very likely have clouted me across the face. And we're engaged to be married. Or we were. I don't know. I know one thing, though. (*Pause*) I've got the wrong sister.

Carol Just because she might not be right for you doesn't mean that . . .

Bob Say what you mean, love. You said yourself we're friends.

Carol Yes, that's just it. We are friends, Bob. And it's been fun.

Bob Aye. You'll go back to college and I'll find meself another job and one of these days we'll pass on the street and you'll say to your university boy friend, "Look, that's the chap that used to be engaged to me sister."

Carol (*upset*) I'm sorry about this, Bob. I'd no idea.

Bob How could you have? Never mind.

Carol And is it really all over between you and Bessie?

Bob Oh, aye. She doesn't know it yet but it is.

Carol If I'd thought that I was coming between you . . .

Bob You haven't. I've told you about Bessie. I knew it long since, but it needed you and all the business with your dad to make me really see what a big mistake I was walking into.

Carol (*with a deep sigh*) Well—I don't suppose you've had time to think about what you're going to do—when you leave Croslands, I mean.

Bob I've been studying accountancy at nights. I shall get another job —some sort of job—and carry on with that till I get some qualifications. It'll be worse for your dad, finding something else at his age.

Carol How's he taken the news? Has he said anything, or is he still not talking to you?

Bob I haven't seen him, love. He hasn't been to work for the last three days.

Carol That's not like him, is it?

Bob No, it isn't. I've allus thought that even if he had a broken leg he'd hobble to work on crutches.

Carol And soon he won't have any work.

Bob He should have a fair old slab of redundancy pay to come, though. He's been at Croslands for donkeys' years.

Carol A lot of good it's done him. I suppose that's how me mam feels. She's been married for thirty-odd years, and a lot of good it's done her.

Bob Thirty years? No wonder it comes over some men when they get to that age.

Carol What?

Bob Well, a feeling like, that it's all slipping by and there's not long left.

Carol You mean the pre-senility virility syndrome.

Bob Do I?

Carol Yes. I've read about it many a time but I've never met it so close to.

Bob If you know the ailment, what about the cure?

Carol That's not so easy.

Bob No. And if it involves a course of cosy chats with a trick-cyclist you can forget it because your dad won't wear it.

Carol Understanding is the first step. And you don't begin to understand until you're prepared to sit down and talk reasonably, and even more important, listen.

Bob And shouting an' bawling only make things worse.

Carol Of course they do.

Bob How do you think you'll measure up as a referee?

Carol I don't know. I'm doing my best.

Bob Aye. They're lucky to have you. Just think, if they'd stopped with your Bessie.

Carol You mustn't get bitter about Bessie, Bob. She has her good points.

Bob Nay, I'm just thinking that if you're an example of the way a strain can improve, your dad aught to get cracking and father a couple more before his pre-senility virility packs up for good.

Carol Oh, yes, you encourage him!

Bob I'm beginning to wonder if there might not be more sense in encouraging than criticizing. I mean, your mam's past childbearing by some way, but your dad's still got a shot or two in his locker. So where does that leave him?

Carol Well, that's . . .

Bob No, don't give me your name for it. Your Bessie's got one that everybody understands.

Carol I can guess what it is, too.

Bob Aye, an' it makes me mad to hear her talk. Anybody 'ud think men were put on the earth to serve women—provide 'em with a home and a family—and then they might as well be castrated.

Carol And what's me mam supposed to do while he sows his last few oats? Turn a blind eye?

Bob It might be better than peering through a telescope.

Carol Is that somebody coming in?

Luther appears in the hall doorway

Dad! You've come. Oh, I am glad!

Luther Is there only you two in?

Carol Mum's round at Marjorie's. Bob'll keep you company. I'll go and fetch her. Then we'll make ourselves scarce.

Luther (*nodding*) All right.

Carol exits to the kitchen

Bob (*turning to Luther*) Luther, I know you don't want to talk to me but . . .

Luther What do you mean?

Bob I suppose you'd rather pretend I wasn't here?

Luther Would I?

Bob (*amazed that Luther has forgotten*) I'm in Coventry, remember?

Luther Nay, that's all forgotten. I've got other things to think about.

Bob Yes, I suppose so.

Luther And life's too short to go on bearing a grudge.

Bob Thanks.

Luther I'll not pretend I'm not pleased to have another man to talk to as well.

Bob Me neither. I'm sorry about the other night.

Luther What do you mean?

Bob I did try to warn you.

Luther How could you know?

Bob I overheard the whole story about your suit going to the cleaners. I should have known that Marjorie and Bessie were cooking up something nasty for you.

Luther Did you, by God! Well, you did try. Don't worry there was nothing you could have done. (*He walks up and down, then stops and looks at Bob*) What you got to say about it all, then?

Bob Nothing.

Luther Nothing? You must have an opinion. Haven't you?

Bob It's p'raps best kept to meself.

Luther That makes a change, anyroad—I'm a disgrace, lad, aren't I? A disgrace to me wife, me daughters, and to meself.

Bob says nothing. Luther suddenly bangs on the table

Well, I don't care! I don't damn' well care! (*He resumes walking up and down*)

Bob Have you heard the news about Croslands?

Luther Aye, it's in tonight's paper.

Bob Aren't you bothered about it?

Luther What can I do about it?

Bob I don't know. I just thought you'd not feel like taking it lying down.

Luther Nay, lad. I know when t'cards are down, like anybody else. You buy the system when you're born into it. And by the time you've reached the age where you can think for yourself—that's if you ever do—it's all gone so deep you've not just economic survival to contend with, you're kicking again morality an' all. An' we're still bringing young 'uns up the same way. Look at our Bessie. She's one of me own an' I must be as much to blame as anybody. But for all her sharp tongue and her noise about thinkin' for herself, she's as big a bloody zombie as ever walked the face of this earth. They call 'em programmes 'at they put into computers, don't they? Well, our Bessie's programmed right down to the grave. Then there's our Marjorie—she's like nowt so much as a contented sow lying in her own muck wi' a litter crawlin' round her. Have you ever been inside her house?

Bob No.

Luther I've never seen it yet when it didn't look like a tip. By God, but this business might ha' gone a bit different if them two hadn't stuck their oars in. You bring your bairns into the world, raise 'em, an' protect 'em, an' before you know where you are you need protecting *from* 'em. Anyway, what does it matter how it comes out, eh? It's still wrong in the beginning, isn't it?

Bob I don't know.

Luther You don't? Wonders never cease! I've found somebody who doesn't think I'm the biggest dirty dog since Bluebeard.

Bob It depends what you do now, doesn't it?

Luther Ah! Ah, ah! Now we're getting to it!

Bob Well, let's say it depends what you want.

Luther I want summat I can't bloody well have, that's what I want. I want things like they were before anybody found out.

Bob I see.

Luther I've capped thee, haven't I, lad?

Bob Aye, you have.

Luther Thought I wa' past it, did you?

Bob I didn't think you were the type.

Luther Ah! There's a type, is there?

Bob I don't know, but I never thought you were it.

Luther Thirty year, plodding nicely along, and then I go an' break out like this. . . . Y'know, I rather cap meself. What do I want to go rockin' t'boat for at my age? An' I wouldn't, y'know, if I hadn't met yon' woman. I'd ha' carred quiet an' just batted me time out.

Bob (*ironically*) I can see the day when you carr quiet, Luther.

Luther Tha puts a lot o' value on a bit o' shout an' blether, lad. Hasn't tha noticed—the further I open me mouth the plainer it is I've no teeth left? It wasn't allus like that. There was a time when I could bite an' draw blood. But that's a long time ago, and I've been taking it lying down for years. (*He pauses and sighs*) An' then I met Ann. Marriage is a funny thing. It can start off as wholesome an' appetizin' as fresh baked bread. Then it gradually turns into last week's mouldy loaf. Don't get me wrong—I'm fond o' Bessie's mother. She's put up wi' me for thirty-two year an' I'll be t'first to admit 'at I've not allus been t'easiest o' men to live wi'. But what does she want out o' me now? Somebody to bring a wage home, put a shelf up, help wi' t'decoratin', keep t'bed warm in cold weather?

Bob Somebody to talk to.

Luther Nay, she talks more to our Bessie an' Marjorie than she ever talks to me.

Bob P'raps you don't listen.

Luther P'raps I don't. P'raps I'm not bloody interested. An' I don't think she is, either. She used to look at me havin' politics like another wife might look at her husband drinking too much or sufferin' from fits. It war a nuisance an' it lost me jobs. She didn't complain—or not often —but neither did she show any sign of understanding.

Bob Does this Mrs Fairchild understand?

Luther I don't know. But you feel she's *interested*. She takes all of you and wants to know what makes you tick. I got shock of me life when I met Ann and she took notice of me.

Bob You were flattered.

Luther I bloody was! And what's wrong wi' that? For the first time in thirty year I began a close relationship with another human being. By God, Bob, I can't tell you how I felt! And if you want to know why I didn't stop an' consider what I was doing I'll tell you—I knew what I was doing and King Dick couldn't ha' stopped me.

Bob She must be a marvellous woman.

Luther Oh, don't talk so wet. She's neither a marvellous woman nor the kind o' slut our Bessie an' Marjorie 'ud make her out to be. She's a warm, intelligent human being 'at happens to be able to give me things I can't get anywhere else. What's more, they're things I've got to have.

Bob Well—there's nobody can stop you having 'em, Luther.

Luther No. Nobody except meself.

Bob Aye. What are you going to do, then?

Luther Does tha think I can deny meself?

Bob Do you think you can deny your conscience?

Luther The way I see things now there's two choices; pack me things or total surrender. An' that's what's come o' them two lasses an' their meddling. I've had my eyes opened in the last few days. I'll not say I didn't bring a lot on myself but by God, I never realized what a nest of vipers I'd raised. And they're all enjoying the situation bar young Carol. Anyway, tha knows now what's waiting for thee if ever tha dares to fly thi kite.

Bob I shan't get married with that intention.

Luther Who does, lad? It takes a funny sort o' feller to go in for all that lyin' an' deceit for t'fun of it. But I'll tell thee summat, though she is me own daughter, I'll be a Dutchman if our Bessie's all a lad like thee needs.

Bob is silent

Tha knows that, does tha?

Bob Maybe I do.

Luther So why don't you tell her?

Bob Your Bessie and me are not on very good terms just now. I don't think we'll be getting wed.

Luther How's that, then?

Bob Well, partly because of you, Luther, an' partly because I—well, as *she* puts it, I tried to take liberties with her.

Luther Did you, by God?

Bob It was nowt at all, really, Luther, I can assure you. I don't want you to be thinking . . .

Luther I know what I think. I reckon if our Bessie thought artificial insemination wa' goin' to become the thing she'd hang on another year or two an' do wi'out a chap altogether.

Bob Nay, Luther, that's a bit hard.

Luther Aye, happen so. After all, artificial insemination doesn't bring a wage home every week, or dig 'garden over. (*Pause*) This lot's makin' me sourer than ever, an' there was a time not so long since when I thought I was going to turn all mellow in me old age.

Bob That'll be the day.

Luther Aye, well. The way I look at it, Bob, I've got about five good years left. Mebbe six or seven, if I'm lucky. Owt after that is just hanging about like that poor bloody dog in there, hoping I shan't make a nuisance of meself. The question now is, how am I going to spend 'em?

Luther goes out through the hall door

Bob now walks up and down himself

Bessie enters from the kitchen

Bob Hello, Bessie.

Bessie "Hello, Bessie!" It's two days since we met and that's all you've got to say?

Bob No, I've quite a lot to say, but this doesn't seem to be the right time.

Bessie I see. I've to wait until you're ready?

Bob I didn't say that.

Bessie (*after a pause*) They say you'll be out of a job by the end of the month.

Bob Aye, I expect so.

Bessie And what are you going to do about it?

Bob Don't know. And at the moment, I don't care. I'm just glad to be rid of the factory.

Bessie And what about us, have you thought about that?

Bob Yes, I have.

Bessie (*seeing the way Bob is behaving and deciding to stake her claim afresh*) Have you noticed anything?

Bob What?

Bessie I'm wearing it again. (*She shows off the ring on her engagement finger*)

Bob Well, that's something else we'll have to talk about.

Bessie What do you mean?

Bob Look, Bessie, you took the ring off because you'd had enough of me. You can't put it back as if nothing has happened.

Bessie Well, as far as I'm concerned, nothing has. Are you saying you won't marry me?

Bob I'm saying we'll have to talk things over calmly.

Bessie (*flaring up*) You're trying to wriggle out of it but you won't. I'll see you don't.

Bob That's it, is it? A fine bloody idea you've got about marriage if you think people have to be forced into it against their will.

Bessie (*bitterly*) You've had nearly three years of my life.

Bob I thought we were sharing, I should have known better.

Bessie One thing I'm glad about. I'm glad I didn't let you get me into bed.

Bob So am I love, so am I.

Marjorie bursts in through the kitchen

Marjorie Where is he?

Bessie Where's who?

Marjorie Me dad. (*To Bob*) Have you seen him?

Bob Yes, I've seen him.

Bessie Why didn't you tell me?

Bob We've only exchanged two words.

Bessie Oh, you men. You'll stick together.

Bob You women don't do so bad.

Bessie Where is he now, then?

Bob He's gone.

Marjorie Oh, damn! If me mam had told me as soon as she came in I could have caught him.

Bob What for?

Marjorie What d'you think for? To tell him what I think about him.

Bob I thought you'd already done that.

Bessie You're in a clever mood tonight, aren't you?

Bob Am I?

Carol comes in with Gladys, who is panting from the exertion of trying to catch Marjorie

Marjorie Bob says he's gone.
Gladys Gone? But he's only just arrived.

Behind this, Bob has caught Carol's eye and signalled Luther's presence with a shake of the head and a quick finger pointed at the ceiling. Bessie catches something out of her eye corner

Bessie What are you two signalling about? Is there something going on between you?
Bob No, there isn't. I'm sorry to say.
Bessie You're sorry? What're you sorry about?
Carol Don't, Bob.
Bob I didn't want to say anything tonight, in front of everybody, but it seems to be the only way to do things in this house. So I'll tell you, Bessie. I prefer your Carol to you, but she doesn't want me.
Bessie So that's what's been going on behind my back.
Gladys You've only yourself to blame, Bessie. You've been playing fast and loose with Bob for long enough.
Bessie I don't expect me own sister to make up to my fiancy.
Bob She hasn't made up to me. I've told you, she doesn't want me. She doesn't want *me* and I don't want *you.*
Bessie So that's all I get for all these years, is it? A polite good-bye. D'you think you can cast me off as easy as that?
Gladys Better now than later. Think yourself lucky he's found out in time.
Bessie I'll thank you to keep out of this, Mother.
Gladys (*her voice rising*) And I'll thank you to keep out of this business with your father. You an' our Marjorie an' all.
Marjorie Why, if it hadn't been for me you'd never have known.
Gladys Aye, an' I might have been a damn' sight better off not knowing. What have I got now for all me knowing except a bellyful of flamin' righteous indignation? And all through your damned meddling!
Bessie Well, that's a fine thing! Blame us now.

Bob motions Carol to slip out and warn Luther

Carol goes through the door to the hall

Bob At least they've made sure you know you're in the right, Mrs Stringer. Like the feller that got knocked down on the zebra crossing.
Bessie Who asked you for your opinion?

Luther enters, followed by Carol

Luther I asked him, only he wouldn't give it to me.
Bessie (*turning to Bob*) Why, you rotten liar. You knew he was still here.
Luther That's right, Bessie, he did. What makes you think you've a right to know every damn' thing 'at goes on in this house?
Bessie Because me mam needs friends, that's why.
Luther One thing's certain: with friends like you an' our Marjorie she doesn't need any bloody enemies.

Bessie She's got 'em, though, hasn't she, with you and that woman?

Luther If your mam an' me are not enemies already it's no fault of your spiteful tongue.

Marjorie That's right, blame everybody but yourself. If you'd played fair none o' this would've happened.

Luther Played fair? Oh, we're playing games now, are we? Well, I'll tell you how t'next round's goin' to be played. It starts wi' Bob takin' Bessie out of here and for a walk down t'street. He's got summat to tell you.

Bessie He's already told me.

Luther Well, listen to him while he tells you again an' happen t'message'll really start to sink in.

Bessie I'm not going anywhere until I know what you . . .

Luther (*thundering*) You're going out of here inside t'next sixty seconds An' if I hear another word out of you I'll tip you over, big as y'are, an' tan your arse.

Gladys Luther, remember the neighbours.

Luther Aye, by God, I'd forgotten about them. We ought to get 'em in an' ask their opinion, didn't we? Or do you think we might get to know what you an' me think, because we haven't yet?

Marjorie We all know what me mam thinks.

Luther No we bloody don't. All we know is what you tell her she ought to think.

Marjorie What all decent people think.

Luther Decent people!

Marjorie Aye, decent people. People who don't carry them things in their pockets.

Luther A pity your Jim didn't.

Marjorie What do you mean! Everyone knows our Kevin were premature.

Bob I didn't know that.

Luther Join the club, lad.

Marjorie I've nothing to reproach myself for.

Luther It must be marvellous to be so flaming righteous.

Marjorie I've always lived a clean and decent life.

Luther Clean? Have you ever really looked at your house—or haven't you time for poking your nose into what doesn't concern you?

Marjorie My mother concerns me.

Luther And a fine way you have of showing it, stirring things up. I can just see you there standing outside that pub in the pouring rain. Keyhole Kate.

Marjorie turns to interrupt, but he goes on

What were you thinking about as you stood there? How much were you thinking about your mother then? I bet you were having a right old gloat. (*He imitates her*) "I've got something on the old devil at last." Well, you've had your fun, now you can have your marching orders. Get back down t'street an' see to your own. That young Kevin was scratching like he had nits when I saw him last week.

Marjorie flies at him, hands up. He holds her off. There is a shocked pause.
Gladys takes Marjorie by the arm and leads her to the kitchen door

Gladys Come on, Marjorie, there's nothing you can do here. You as well,
Bessie.

Marjorie exits

Bob I'll wait for you outside, Bessie.
Bessie I don't need you to wait for me.
Bob Just as you like. (*He goes to the door*) Good-bye, Mrs Stringer, Luther.
I hope—I hope things turn out all right.
Gladys Cheerio, Bob.
Bob 'Bye, Carol, see you around.
Carol Yes, good-bye, Bob.
Luther Aye, so long, lad. Be good.

Bob goes

You're a daft bitch, Bessie.
Bessie (*shaken*) I beg your pardon.
Luther Tryin' to make a doormat out of a chap like him. That pride o'
yours 'ull be poor company for you in your old age.
Bessie At least I'll be able to rely on it, which is more than I can say for
most men I've seen. (*She takes her coat to exit via the kitchen, then turns
to Carol*) And you'd better come as well.

Bessie exits

Carol looks at her parents in turn

Carol I'll go upstairs.

Carol exits

Luther subsides into a chair

Gladys I've told you before about getting worked up like that. You'll
have a stroke afore you're finished.
Luther It'll take more than them to finish me off.
Gladys So, you've come back? Has she had enough of you?
Luther I've not been living with her, if that's what you mean.
Gladys Oh, of course she'd have her reputation to consider.
Luther There's a difference between visiting a woman living on her own
and staying several nights.
Gladys I wouldn't have thought such niceties would have bothered her.
Luther That's only part of it. One thing marriage has taught me. When
two people live together they put chains round one another. An' what's
t'point in throwing off one set only to put another lot on?
Gladys I suppose it's all right in theory. I thought if you cared about
somebody you'd *want* to live with them, get to know them.

Luther Well, we've lived together for over thirty years and a fat lot we know about each other. You didn't even know I was having an affair for the past year till our Marjorie found out.

Gladys So I'm to blame for that, am I? I'm to blame for your cunning in hiding it? How was I supposed to notice when there's been nothing like that in our lives since our Carol was born. Tell me you've been off with dozens of women and I'm stupid for not noticing. You're selfish, Luther.

Luther Happen that's how it looks.

Gladys (*after a pause*) Well, I don't know what you've got in mind, but if you'll agree not to see that woman again, I'm willing to have you back. But you'll have to patch things up with Marjorie and Bessie. I can't stand family squabbles.

Luther Patch things up with them two?

Gladys They're your own flesh and blood, Luther, and you are in the wrong.

Luther Does that give 'em a right to behave like savages?

Gladys It's their way. And there's plenty round here who'd back 'em in what they did.

Luther Aye, I'd happen have laughed meself if it had been somebody else. An' if we've only moved that far out o' t'cave I must be as much to blame as anybody, because I helped bring 'em up. (*A pause*) I've been doing it wrong for years. I've known it. I've watched meself. Because for the life in me I somehow couldn't do it right. And it's been killing me. There comes a time when you realize that you on your own can't cure your mistakes—can't wipe 'em out—because you've bred 'em into somebody else's bones. They parade in front of you every day, taunting you; and when you rile at 'em they answer you back. Aye, I'm in the wrong, all right; and them two have only one thought in their heads— to beat me to me knees till I crawl back here an' eat dirt for the rest of me days.

Gladys An' you won't do that.

Luther I will not.

Gladys So what is there left to talk about?

Luther Is that what you want an' all, Gladys?

Gladys I hoped you might be able to see it different.

Luther An' if I can't?

Gladys You're not much good to me like that.

Luther No, I thought not. (*A pause*) Tha're going to have to let me go, aren't tha, lass?

Gladys There's no lettin' here. You know where t'door is.

Luther Ey, but I dislike seein' thee like this.

Gladys Not enough, though, eh?

Luther I never wanted it to come to this.

Gladys You shouldn't have been so careless, then.

Luther Mebbe, at bottom of me, I did want it to come out. Happen I couldn't really abide the way I wa' carryin' on.

Gladys It's not your way, is it?

Luther No, it's not my way. I've allus liked having things straight an' out in t'open. Whether it offended folk or not.

Gladys Well, you've offended me.

Luther Aye, I know. But you see, time's gettin' on an' there's summat it seems 'at I must have.

Gladys An' yon' woman's got it?

Luther I think she can point t'way for me.

Gladys I see.

Luther (*after a pause*) I'll see you get your money. Don't worry about that.

Gladys You'll be needing another job.

Luther There'll be a bit of redundancy pay to tide me over.

Gladys I shall be down at the post office first thing tomorrow to see about my share of that account.

Luther Well, that's your right.

Gladys Aye. So—you're going to pack your things?

Luther I have done already. T'case is in t'passage.

Gladys When'll you be back for the rest?

Luther I've got all I need. There's not that much that's personal belongings when you think about it.

Gladys So you won't be coming back?

Luther No, it's best not.

Gladys (*after a pause*) You'll be wanting to be off, then?

Luther I don't like to leave you like this.

Gladys No, I dare say you won't find it as easy to walk through that door as you did last time.

Luther I couldn't have left it like that, though.

Gladys Besides, you needed your things.

Luther Give us a bit o' credit, love. I shall miss you. We've had a good long innings.

Gladys And in less than a fortnight it's all over. You'd better get off. Hanging about here, talking sentimental won't make it any easier.

Luther You'll be all right. You'll have the house and your money. There'll be our Bessie for company and our Marjorie popping round like she's allus done. All you'll miss is my bad temper and you'll soon get over that.

Gladys (*turning her head away*) Go, will you. Get yourself out.

Luther gets up and approaches her. She shrugs off the hand he ventures to lay on her shoulder

Leave me be and go!

Luther goes into the passage and returns with the suitcase, he turns round at the door

Luther So long, then. Take care. I er, I'll drop you a line.

No answer. Luther goes out

Gladys sits for a long time with her head bowed. Eventually she gets up and

*takes her sewing-basket from a cupboard. She sews buttons on a blouse.
Carol comes in from the hall*

Carol He's gone, then.

Gladys Didn't you see him?

Carol At the door. He gave me a kiss and said "so long". He had a suitcase with him.

Gladys Aye. He says he won't be coming back.

Carol It didn't do any good, then, me trying to get you together?

Gladys It doesn't look like it, does it?

Carol You did talk, though, didn't you? I mean, it wasn't just recrimina-
tions.

Gladys Oh, no, there were few hard words. I did call him selfish once.

Carol (*after a pause*) Well, that's that.

Gladys Aye.

Carol I don't know how you can sit there sewing and talk about it so
calmly. As if you didn't care.

Gladys Because I have no option, lass. And your father in his own way
had none either. What good's a feller 'at's had his nose rubbed in it? I
don't want a man at any price. I can remember your father when he was a
fighting-cock, when he stood up for what he believed in an' suffered for it.

Carol Did you ever understand what all that was about?

Gladys No, not really. It allus seemed to me 'at we could have had a
pleasant life if he'd only curb himself a bit. But I was his wife, an' understand him or not it was my place to make a home for him.

Carol (*bitterly*) Until he was tired of it and fancied something else.

Gladys Where's that understanding we were talking about before? What
does it amount to? Me forgiving him and him coming back, is that as
far as it goes?

Carol I wanted to see you work something out.

Gladys We have worked it out. And he's gone. For now.

Carol For now? You don't think he's gone for good, then?

Gladys Nay, all's not over between your father an' me. I know a thing or
two about him 'at yon other woman doesn't, an' there'll come a time
when he'll need that. It's all right her sayin' she wants him to be free,
not to put any more chains on as she calls it. But that's what a relationship between a man and woman is. A man wants a place where he can
come home, not talking much maybe, but with somebody there to see
to his needs. Your father's lived too long like that to settle to any other
way. Our Marjorie says that woman makes him laugh. But nobody
laughs forever. He'll be back. I can remember when your grandfather
—my father—used to come in from t'pit, bone-weary an' black as night.
Your grandmother used to ladle hot water into t'sink from the fireside
boiler. Then he'd strip to t'waist an' brace himself with his hand on the
sink whilst she washed his back. All with hardly a word.

Carol But that's the sort of thing a mother does for her sons.

Gladys Ey, lass, but you've still a lot to learn about men.

CURTAIN

FURNITURE AND PROPERTY LIST

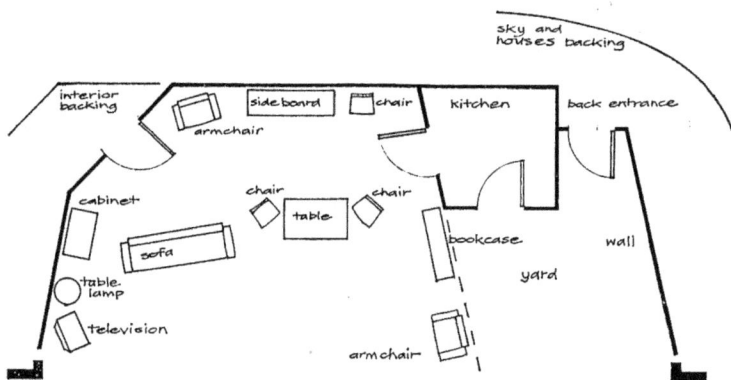

ACT I

SCENE 1

On stage: Sofa. *On it:* cushions
           2 armchairs
           3 small chairs
           Sideboard. *On it:* radio, pile of plates, tray
           Bookcase. *In it:* books, magazines
           Cabinet. *Over it:* mirror. *In it:* sewing basket with blouse, buttons,
              cotton, thread
           Occasional table. *On it:* table lamp
           Table. *On it:* cloth, 3 knives, 3 forks, 3 spoons, 3 glasses, 3 small
              plates, 3 soup plates, serving spoon, vase of plastic daffodils,
              condiments, etc.
           Television set
           Carpet
           Hearthrug (set down c)

Off stage: Newspaper (**Luther**)
           Pot of stew and dumplings (**Gladys**)
           Suit on hanger (**Marjorie**)
           Packet of contraceptives (**Marjorie**)

Personal: **Bessie:** engagement ring
           Bob: matches
           Jack: cigarettes

SCENE 2

Strike: Newspaper
              Plates

Set: Vacuum-cleaner on stage
              Luther's shoes on hearthrug

Off stage: Duffel bag (**Carol**)
              Tray of tea-things: 3 cups, 3 saucers, 3 spoons, milk, sugar, teapot

Personal: **Bessie:** purse with coins

ACT II

SCENE 1

Strike: Hoover cleaner

Off stage: Tray of tea-things: 4 cups, 4 saucers, 4 spoons, milk, sugar, teapot
              Sample case with "foundations" (**Ann**)
              Scissors (**Bessie**)

SCENE 2

Strike: Tea-things

Set: 2 cups, 2 saucers, 2 spoons, milk, sugar, teapot on table

Off stage: Tray (**Carol**)
              Suitcase (**Luther**)

LIGHTING PLOT

Property fittings required: table or standard lamp, pendant, practical plug for
      Hoover
Interior. A living-room. The same scene throughout

ACT I, SCENE 1 Evening
To open: Pendant and general interior lighting on

Cue 1	**Luther** switches off lights *Black-Out*	(Page 9)
Cue 2	**Bessie** switches on lights *Snap on pendant and interior lighting*	(Page 9)
Cue 3	**Bessie:** ". . . but she didn't want to." *TV set warms up*	(Page 10)
Cue 4	**Bessie** switches on lamp *Bring up table lamp by TV*	(Page 10)
Cue 5	**Bessie** switches off pendant *Snap out pendant and general lighting*	(Page 10)
Cue 6	**Bessie** switches on pendant *Snap on pendant and general lighting*	(Page 11)
Cue 7	**Bob** switches off TV *Fade television spot*	(Page 14)

ACT I, SCENE 2 Morning
To open: General effect of daylight

Cue 8	**Marjorie:** ". . . we might never have known!" *Fade to Black-Out*	(Page 32)

ACT II, SCENE 1 Evening
To open: Pendant and lamp on
No cues

ACT II, SCENE 2 Evening
To open: As Scene 1
No cues

EFFECTS PLOT

ACT I

Scene 1

Scene 2

ACT II

Scene 1

Scene 2

No cues